TRADITIONAL GARDEN WOODWORK

TRADITIONAL GARDEN WOODWORK

Peter Holland

WARD LOCK

A WARD LOCK BOOK

First paperback edition 1995
First published in the UK 1994
by Ward Lock
Wellington House
125 Strand
LONDON
WC2R 0BB

An imprint of the Cassell Group

Distributed in the United States
by Sterling Publishing Co., Inc.
387 Park Avenue South, New York, NY 10016-8810

Distributed in Australia
by Capricorn Link (Australia) Pty Ltd
2/13 Carrington Road, Castle Hill NSW 2154

A British Library Cataloguing in Publication Data block for this book may be obtained
from the British Library

ISBN 0-7063-7451-7

Typeset by Method Limited, Epping, Essex.

Printed in Great Britain by The Bath Press, Avon

CONTENTS

ACKNOWLEDGEMENTS

Many thanks to George Court and Ray and Rita Hodges in whose delightful gardens some of the pieces were photographed. Also to Dave Lees who provided helpful ornithological data.

DISCLAIMER

While every care has been taken to ensure that the information given here is accurate, readers should check their dimensions as work proceeds to see that they comply with the cutting lists. Timber as bought may not be exactly the same as these lengths, and is sold by the metre. The lists are to indicate the lengths used. (Measure twice, cut once.) It may be more economical to combine several projects to avoid wastage to the nearest metre.

Neither the author nor the publishers can be responsible for accidents, injury or spoilt work.

Introduction

WOODWORK in someone else's garden may bring to mind those splintered ends of rustic poles joined by rusty nails, or a rotting seat that wobbles. Such nightmares were probably produced by someone who had nothing but enthusiasm, a blunt saw and a large hammer. This book will show you how to use woodwork creatively, with a full range of techniques, to enhance and bring real individuality to your garden.

You do not have to be a cabinet-maker to build the items. The joints are quite simple, and each new one is described in detail in step-by-step instructions in the succeeding projects. They need not be vastly expensive either: following the instructions given, the wood – easily available from the local woodyard in standard sizes, or from DIY shops – is used economically.

There are thirty-one items for you to build under the eighteen main project headings. For these you can use mostly easy-to-obtain, easy-to-work pine, and not exotic hardwoods or those from non-sustainable sources.

As you might expect, these pieces of woodwork will not be so durable as those made from teak, oak or other hardwoods. But, then, maybe you are not interested in producing heirlooms. You may simply want to improve your skills without expensive mistakes, and you may not want to take everything with you should you move home.

The joints are designed to resist weathering. They are additionally protected by using really waterproof glue, such as epoxy or polyester resin, which is obtainable at DIY shops (in the car-repair section).

With reasonable maintenance, and adequate application of the right types of wood-preservative, varnish/stain or paint, the life of garden furniture, fittings and features might be as long as, say, external pine-cladding on a house.

Clearly, the larger items described in these pages do not come under the 'kitchen-table workbench' heading, but a garden shed of not less than 2.5 × 2 metres (8 x 6 ft) will accommodate most of the construction stages of all but those pieces that have to be built as garden fixtures, such as pergolas, and large trellis or fencing items. A garage is more than adequate and, of course, is ideal for storing timber alongside, or even under, the car, between sessions of woodworking in the shed.

Most gardens, large or small, will benefit from the introduction of woodwork features. Here is a chance both to improve your woodworking experience by taking it in a new direction and, at the same time, to get inspiration for your very own woodwork designs, for your garden and those of your friends.

WHAT YOU NEED

JOINTS AND TOOLS

There are complex woodworking joints involved in making household furniture and there are simple ones. In the type of woodwork needed for garden projects, only simple joints are used. The making of each one will be described separately in detail, and then as they come up in the projects themselves.

Fig. 1 shows a typical group of joints and Table 1 (see page 15) notes the tools needed in actually forming them. The entire range of tools need not be wide; indeed, most households already have such items such as handsaws, hand-drills, chisels, screwdrivers and hammers. Consider whether these will be right for the work, or what else to buy to make a proper job of it.

Fig. 1

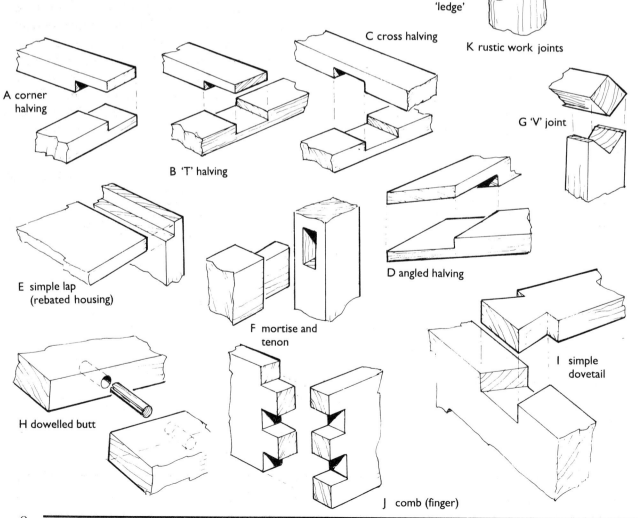

saddle

'V'

'ledge'

K rustic work joints

A corner halving

B 'T' halving

C cross halving

D angled halving

E simple lap (rebated housing)

F mortise and tenon

G 'V' joint

H dowelled butt

I simple dovetail

J comb (finger)

Almost everything needs the following short, initial marking-out kit (Fig. 2).

RULE

Not just a steel tape (which twangs about). For small, precise measurements, use a carpenter's rule, usually 1 metre (3 ft) long. Most are marked in metric and imperial divisions – useful when checking sizes given in only either millimetres or inches and converting them to whichever you find easiest to work with. Never use it to score against; a straight metal strip is better.

PENCIL

Some people use a ballpoint pen, which then clogs up with sawdust. Some use a felt-tip pen, which wears down, leaving too thick a line, which is also difficult to sand clean.

An HB lead is the right grade. Special carpenter's pencils have a large-section oval lead, which does not wear down so easily as the drawing variety. This does not mean that it need not be sharpened to a good chisel point. Mark areas that have to be cut away with crosses or scribble.

MARKING KNIFE

Fat lines do not make for accurate marking out, so really precise lines, where cuts are to go, are drawn by cutting the surface with a marking knife.

MARKING AWL

Use this thin, pointed tool to mark hole centres and to prick through templates. Do not confuse it with a bradawl, which has a slightly wider tip, chisel-pointed to cut across the grain, so that fixing pins do not split thin wood.

CARPENTER'S SQUARES

There are two types: a 'try square', for true 90-degree checking and marking; and the adjustable 'sliding bevel', with which different angles can be marked. Set the latter from the template in Fig. 3, or from a drawing protractor.

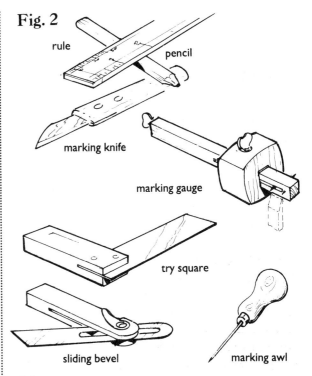

Fig. 2

rule

pencil

marking knife

marking gauge

try square

sliding bevel

marking awl

MARKING GAUGE

This traditional tool enables you to scribe accurate lines parallel to the edge of the wood. It has a set of steel points in a wood handle, and a block which can be slid along and locked to run against the edge of the wood. The point marks the line. One of two points on the other side is adjustable so that two parallel lines can be marked for mortises and grooves.

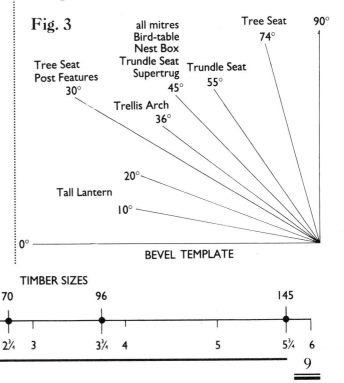

Fig. 3

all mitres
Bird-table
Nest Box

Tree Seat 90°

Tree Seat 74°

Tree Seat Post Features 30°

Trundle Seat Supertrug 45°

Trundle Seat 55°

Trellis Arch 36°

Tall Lantern

20°

10°

0°

BEVEL TEMPLATE

TIMBER SIZES

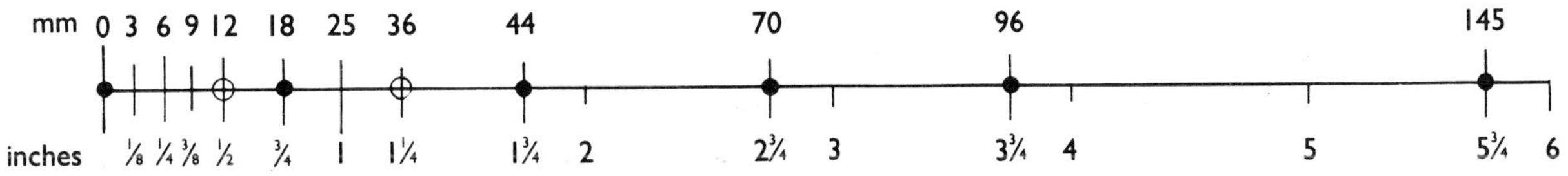

mm	0 3 6 9 12	18	25	36	44	70	96	145
inches	⅛ ¼ ⅜ ½	¾	1	1¼	1¾ 2	2¾ 3	3¾ 4	5 5¾ 6

Now, do you have the right type of tools? Fig. 4 shows a selection of saws.

HANDSAWS

Your large handsaw is probably what is known as a combination saw. This means that it will cut large-section wood, both along the grain (known as rip-sawing) and across the grain (a cross-cut). Rip-saw teeth are larger than cross-cut types, and shave the wood rather than chopping it.

Fig. 4

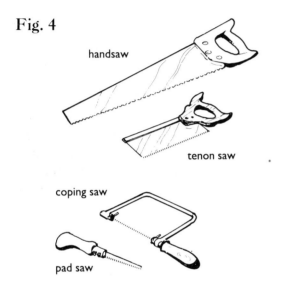

If a large-tooth saw is used for cuts across the grain, it produces a very ragged finish, and probably tries to dance about when the cut is started. The combination-tooth-type, however, may have about eight points per 25 mm (1 in). It takes longer to make a rip-cut, but should cut thin plywood as well.

TENON SAW

The accurate cutting of joints demands a small tooth – say twelve or more points per 25 mm (1 in). The blade is short and wide and has a reinforcing strip along the back to keep it perfectly straight and rigid.

COPING SAW

This is another traditional tool. It has a fine, thin blade tensioned in a frame, but is not to be confused with a fretsaw, which is intended for light work. Its blade can be turned to face sideways or forward, which makes it ideal for cutting curved lines and

for getting into tight, enclosed corners. At a pinch, a small keyhole saw or a pad saw may be used instead, but the blade is wider and needs to be handled carefully if it is to remain straight. As will be seen later, a couple of power-tools may do the job of several of these hand-tools.

CHISELS

The only chisels needed for the projects are 6, 9, 12, 18 and 25 mm (¼, ⅜, ½, ¾ and 1 in). Most modern chisels have chamfered sides, but you may have some with a rectangular section. These are known as 'firmers'. Even thicker and stronger are those specially intended for chopping out mortises. The chamfer-edged types are useful for allowing the chisel to cut into narrow-angled spaces, such as are made in dovetail joints (Fig. 5).

Fig. 5

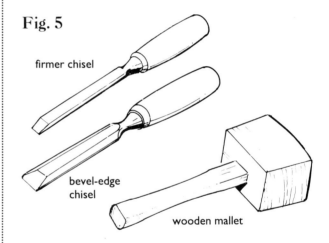

WOODEN MALLET

If you have wooden-handled chisels, the traditional wooden mallet (also shown in Fig. 5) has to be used, to save damage to the ends. Never use a hammer on a wooden handle. In any case, there is more control when the larger head of a wood mallet is used. Some manufacturers illustrate metal hammers in use with their hard plastic-handled chisels, but I still use a wood mallet on these. Heavy thumps are no substitute for proper sharpening and honing of the chisel edge.

PLANES

Two planes are shown in Fig. 6. A smoothing plane has a long, flat under-surface (called the sole). This plane is to give a level finish to sawn surfaces, to remove wood evenly with the grain and to chamfer or round edges. A 230-mm (9-in) type should suffice for these tasks.

Fig. 6

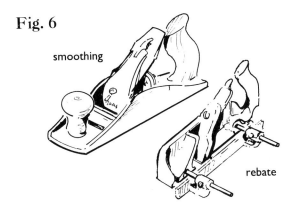

smoothing

rebate

If you do not intend to use power-tools such as a router, you will need a rebate plane. This cuts a long recess in the edge of the wood, into which another piece may fit. You can also buy planes which will do both jobs, but see that the shavings do not get jammed at the edge, by taking thin cuts.

SHARPENING STONE

Sharp-edged tools like chisels and the blades (irons) of planes must be kept sharp. Forget power-grinders for the moment; tools as bought should be ready to use and be kept sharp (there is a separate chapter dealing with sharpening). For now, choose a flat carborundum oilstone or a whetstone, each complete with protective box (Fig. 7). It should have medium and fine sides.

Fig. 7

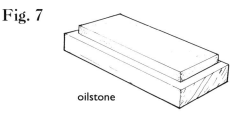

oilstone

SCREWDRIVERS

You can never have too many different sizes of screwdriver. The important thing is to have one that fits the recess in the head of the screw perfectly. This may sound obvious, but look at Fig. 8. This shows what happens when the wrong size is used.

Fig. 8

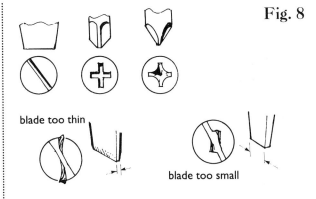

blade too thin

blade too small

HAND-DRILL

Shown in Fig. 9, it is fine for small jobs and small holes, and essential in confined spaces or for tiny holes if your electric drill is a man-sized weighty chunk.

You may have a hand-brace (also shown). This is for slow boring jobs. It is quiet, though, and will even work with a tungsten carbide bit for drilling walls for fixings, and with helical auger bits for large holes in wood. It is not essential if you have a two-speed electric drill.

Fig. 9

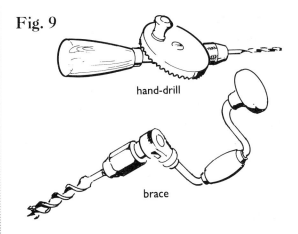

hand-drill

brace

COUNTERSINK

This is a hand-tool used for recessing countersunk-headed (csk) screws (Fig. 10). There is also a countersink drill bit for doing the same job. You need only one or the other.

Fig. 10

DRILL BITS

There is a range of twist drill bits specially designed for woodwork. Their tips are shown in Fig. 11. They make a clean, straight hole, but they need to be taken care of, and when resharpened those spurs need to be retained. Large holes 12 to 25 mm (½ to 1 in) in diameter can be made with flat bits (Fig. 12). Use these only in an electric drill.

Fig. 11

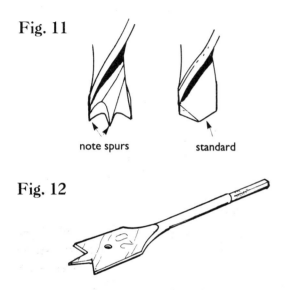

note spurs   standard

Fig. 12

HOLE SAW

Even larger holes can be made with this accessory to electric drills (Fig. 13). It has a set of curved hacksaw-like blades in various diameters from 30 to 60 mm (1¼ to 2½ in).

Fig. 13

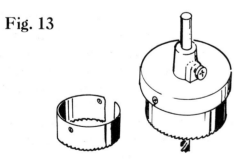

HAMMERS

There is not much nailing to be done, but you should have the hammers shown in Fig. 14: the claw type, which also removes temporary nails holding a joint that cannot be clamped; and a Warrington type, for small nails and getting into corners.

Fig. 14

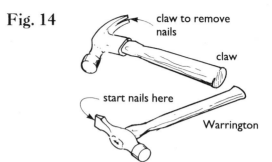

claw to remove nails

claw

start nails here

Warrington

MALLET

In keeping with the garden theme, a mallet is necessary for walloping posts into the ground. You will need a 2-kg (4-lb) type. This must never be used for persuading woodwork chisels to work!

CRAMPS

You will need several 'G' cramps, and a 'hold down', to hold wood on the bench-top while working, and some joints while the glue sets. If you already have a couple of sash cramps, these will help to edge-join wide boards, or to hold joints in frames. However, as will be described later, they need not be bought specially. Fig. 15 shows the three examples.

Fig. 15

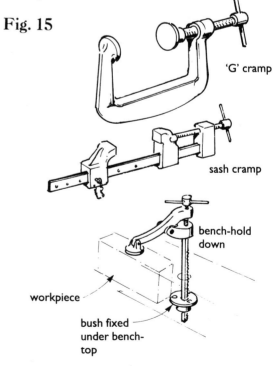

'G' cramp

sash cramp

bench-hold down

workpiece

bush fixed under bench-top

SANDING BLOCK

You can make this yourself if you do not already have one (Fig. 16).

Fig. 16

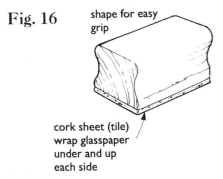

shape for easy grip

cork sheet (tile) wrap glasspaper under and up each side

VICE

If you have a workbench, it probably has a vice. If it is a metalwork type, its use for woodwork is restricted by the area of grip it offers and you will need to fit it with wood-jaw facings to avoid damage to the job (Fig. 17). However, most of the projects in this book can be built with the aid of a 'Workmate' or similar portable bench.

Fig. 17

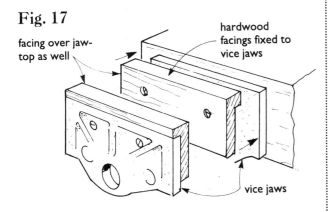

facing over jaw-top as well

hardwood facings fixed to vice jaws

vice jaws

BENCH HOOK

Make this yourself, as in Fig. 18, to restrain wood while sawing. It hooks over the bench edge.

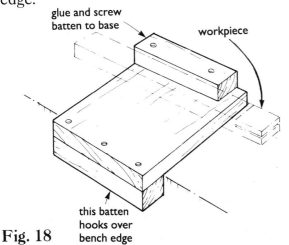

glue and screw batten to base

workpiece

this batten hooks over bench edge

Fig. 18

BENCH STOP

Another home-made aid, this prevents wood sliding when you plane it on the bench (Fig. 19).

Fig. 19

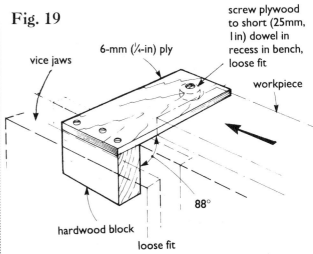

screw plywood to short (25mm, 1in) dowel in recess in bench, loose fit

6-mm (¼-in) ply

vice jaws

workpiece

hardwood block

loose fit

88°

ADDING POWER

The preceding list covers most possibilities, but a number of the traditional hand-tools can be omitted if versatile power-tools are available (see Table 1, page 15).

Power-tools speed things up and in some cases help you to improve accuracy. The most important ones are shown in Fig. 20 (overleaf), and tips on their use are given later in the book.

ELECTRIC DRILL

Choose one with two or variable speeds and a chuck capacity of at least 9 mm (⅜ in). If it has an optional 'hammer' facility, fixings to walls are easier. Some types are reversible and have electronic speed control: you can drive screws or remove them as well.

The flat bits and hole saws make short work of large holes, and some accessories like jigsaws, circular saws and sanding discs eliminate all but the most delicate work. You may prefer to buy self-contained jigsaws and sander tools as they are easier to hold.

PORTABLE ELECTRIC CIRCULAR SAW

The drill-sawing accessories are of necessity small and the method of holding them while in use is not always comfortable. Most electric saws have a tilt facility for cutting at

Fig. 20

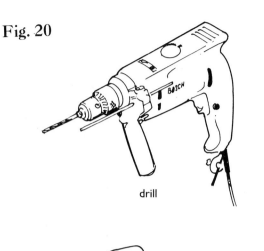

drill

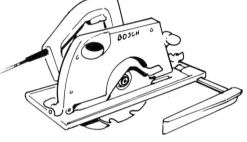

circular saw

jigsaw

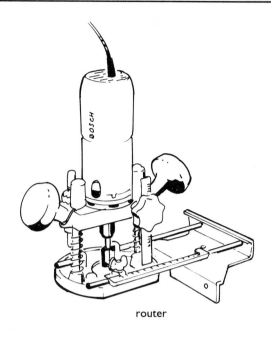

router

ROUTER

Some might manage without it, but for accuracy this is ideal for shaping edges, making joints and removing sections of wood to an accurate depth. It accepts a variety of cutters which will produce straight-sided edges, slots, curved mouldings, 'V'-shaped grooves and rounded channels. It has a depth (plunge) control. Accessories include several types of guide and an adjustable fence.

Finally, there are optional extras. These are shown in Fig. 21.

POWER PLANE

This reduces the thickness of wood fast, but as most of the smooth wood in the projects comes ready-planed, 'planed all round' (PAR), this is a time-saving purchase only for those who want to use lower-cost 'sawn' timber.

BELT SANDER

This is a super tool to use, levelling and shaping at high speed. It is faster than an orbital sander, and the resultant surface is superior to that produced by a sanding disc.

For each project, where appropriate, a list of specific tools and a cutting list have been

an angle and an adjustable depth control. There is also a fence accessory to control an even width of cut. Your average saw has a combination-type blade, some with tungsten carbide tooth tips.

JIGSAW

If there is a curve to cut or a corner to get into, the electric jigsaw with a variety of blades is a versatile tool. It will, at a pinch, replace all the handsaws, but for accuracy it needs to have a guide to cut straight, and for this task the jigsaw is much slower than a circular saw.

Fig. 21

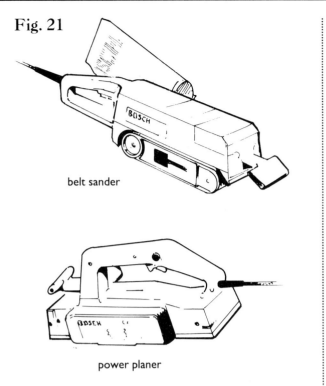

belt sander

power planer

provided. Obviously, these are to be used in conjunction with a basic marking-out kit, glue, screws and nails, and glasspaper, as the instructions indicate. Finishes can be used as you choose. In the illustrations, the piece of wood that is being worked upon is always referred to as the 'workpiece', so as not to be confused with packing pieces and jigs.

Table 1 shows which projects offer scope for the use of power-tools.

Note: Not all power-tools rated for domestic use may be suitable for the workload imposed by building the full list of projects in this book. However, all these pieces are within the capability of the Bosch range of DIY tools described.

TABLE I

Note All items can be made with hand-tools. The ○ symbol indicates that power-tools can be used to replace hand-tools.

Cost	Skill	Projects	BUTT	HALVING	MORTISE AND TENON	DOVETAIL	REBATED HOUSING	HANDSAW	TENON SAW	COPING SAW	CHISELS	SCREWDRIVERS	HAMMERS	DRILL	DRILL	CIRCULAR SAW	JIGSAW	ROUTER	SANDER
★★★	★	Tricks with Trellis – Peephole Trellis	●					●	●	○							○	●	
★	★	Two Nest Boxes – Open, Gabled, plus Bird Feeder	●				●	●	●		●	●	●	●	○	○			
★	★★	Bird-table			●			●	●	○	●	●	●	●	○			●	○
★★	★	Planter Pair	●					●			●	●	●	●	○	○			●
★★★★	★	Picnic Bench		●			●		●		●	●		●	●	○		○	●
★★	★★	Fence Tips: Four Gates – Tall, Small, Trellis, Five-Bar		●	●				●		●	●	●	●	○	●	●	●	
★★	★★	Two Lanterns – Post, Pyramid, plus Plinths	●	●					●	○	●	●		●	○	○	●	○	●
★★	★★	Supertrug – plus a matching basket		●		○	●	○	●	○	●			●	●		○	●	●
★	★★	Post Feature		●	●			○	●	○	●	●		●	●			●	●
★	★	Garden Shelves		●			●	●	●		●	●		●	○	○			
★★	★★	Garden Tool Store		●			●	●	●		●	●	●	●	○	○			
☆★★	★★	Three Arches – Rustic, Braced, Trellis	●	●				●	●		●	●	●	○	●			○	●
☆★★★	★★☆	Three Pergolas – Lean-to, Long, Curved		●	●			●	●		●	●	●		●	●	●		
★★	★★★	Pegged Tenon Planter		●	●			○	●	○	●	●		○	●			○	●
★★★	★★★★★	Garden Bench			●				○		●	●		○				●	●
★★★★★	★★★★★	Gazebo		●	●			●	○		●	●	●	○	●	●	●	●	●
★★★★	★★★	Tree Seat (for a border tree)		●					○		●	●		●	●	●			●
★★	★★★	Gardener's Trundle Seat			●		●	○	●	○	●	●		●	○		○	●	●

JOINTS · TOOLS · IMPORTANT POWER-TOOLS

Gardeners' Woodwork Tips

THERE HAVE PROBABLY been many odd jobs around the garden where you needed to use woodwork of a very basic kind. Perhaps you undertook them without even realizing that they might be done more easily or more permanently. Here are a few tips which will perhaps provide inspiration.

SMALL POSTS AND PEGS

Naturally, wood can be driven into the ground more easily when it has a point at the bottom, but some people simply cut one side only. This gives the point a lopsided appearance – the post creeps to one side as it is driven in, or leans over. That wood-saving diagonal cut is the culprit (Fig. 1).

Suppose the wood splits, or has an untidy, frayed top? Do not hit it directly. Hold a wider piece across the top and hit that.

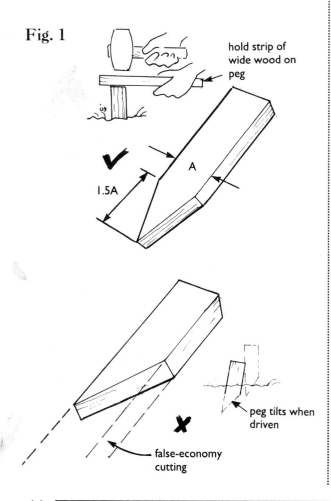

Fig. 1

hold strip of wide wood on peg

1.5A
A

peg tilts when driven

false-economy cutting

PATH EDGES

It is customary to form a hard edge to contain gravel, concrete or grass when making paths or steps. Pegs support the edge strips of, say, 80 × 25-mm (3 × 1-in) sawn wood on edge. These go on the outside of the path and are nailed into the strips.

Push a board up to the strip and stand on it as you nail; otherwise the peg will be loosened (Fig. 2).

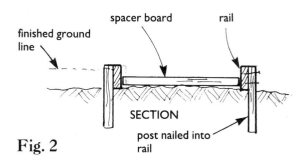

spacer board   rail

finished ground line

SECTION

post nailed into rail

Fig. 2

Curved edges are often made by sawing part-way through the strips on the inside of the curve. If you saw on the outside instead, the wood may break when bent (Fig. 3). Really sharp bends are best made with two or three strips of exterior plywood laminated dry, on edge. Each bends easily, so the pegs are not forced out of line (Fig. 4).

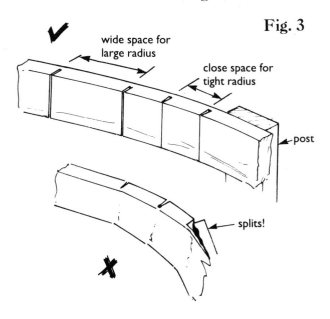

Fig. 3

wide space for large radius

close space for tight radius

post

splits!

Fig. 4

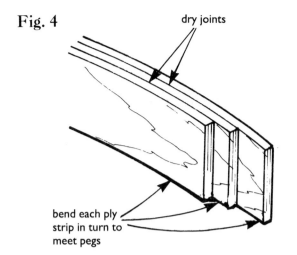

dry joints

bend each ply
strip in turn to
meet pegs

TIDY POTS

On patios or in corners, it is convenient to arrange a floral display in a series of small tubs and pots. Unfortunately, it is often the case that some of these are plastic, others do not match, and who wants to look at humble plastic pots anyway?

Measure the height of the deepest container, arrange smaller ones on bricks to the same level, then enclose the whole group in a serpentine wall of rough wood offcuts, stapled to a couple of lengths of thick galvanized fence wire behind. Allow tiny gaps, so that the wall can be made to bend into concave pot arrangements (see Fig. 5). You can have screening walls which vary in height to suit similar variations in the height of displays. It is so quick to swap pots around as new plants come into flower.

In winter the 'wall' can be used flat, to protect soft lawns when wheeling heavy barrows, or rolled up to save space, or put around delicate plants as a windbreak that will not blow away. Quite tall versions of this wall (1 m/3 ft 3 in high) will need a third wire. Fix the loops to screws in a fence or wall.

Fig. 5

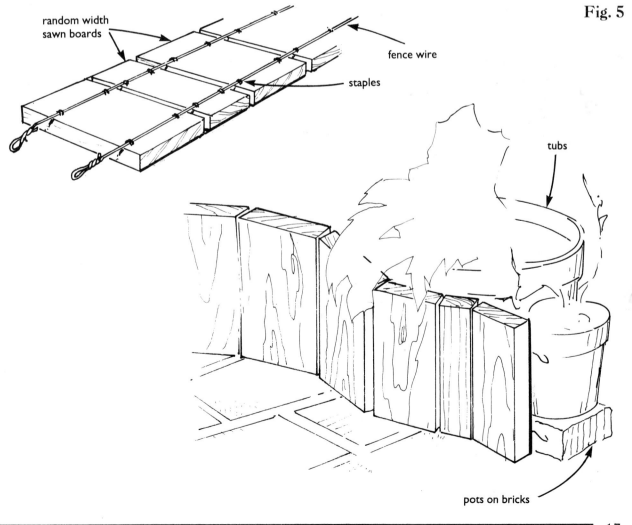

random width
sawn boards

fence wire

staples

tubs

pots on bricks

POST-FIXING

Some features have single posts, so a word here about fixing will not come amiss. Perhaps you would simply point and drive them into the ground firmly enough to withstand the winter gales. But some features are not designed to be walloped in.

A softwood post, even when well soaked in preservative, will rot after some years in the ground or set in concrete. Some remission can be gained by slipping it into a piece of square plastic rainwater pipe and sealing it with bitumen, before setting it in concrete or in a hardcore-filled hole (Fig. 6).

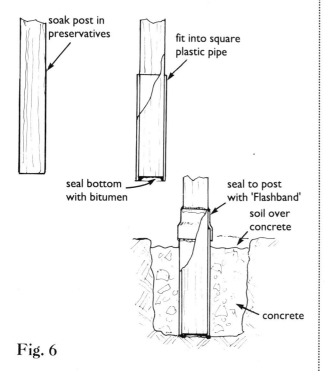

soak post in preservatives

fit into square plastic pipe

seal bottom with bitumen

seal to post with 'Flashband'

soil over concrete

concrete

Fig. 6

MOBILE POSTS

Suppose you wish to take a post-mounted feature down for the winter, or change its position in the garden ... Concrete is awfully permanent; wood will eventually rot. Why not invest in a fence-repair spike? This is a long, strong steel spike with a socket on top. You clamp the post into this with bolts. Come winter or removals, it can be unclamped. The metal stump is not pretty, but it can be hidden under a false-bottomed tub (Fig. 7). A tub standing on bricks gives a similar effect and you can make a dummy sleeve to slide down (as in Fig. 8), or have plants around it when in use.

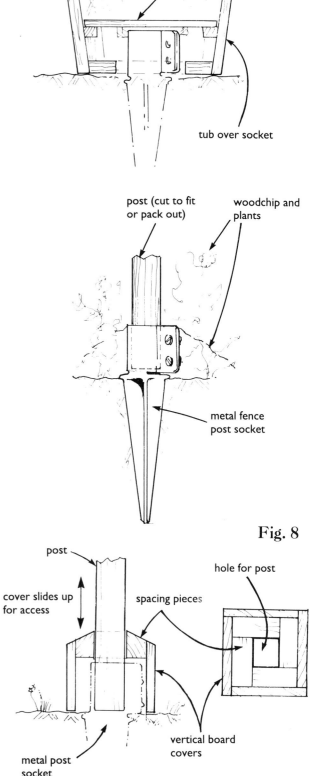

Fig. 7

post withdrawn

false bottom

tub over socket

post (cut to fit or pack out)

woodchip and plants

metal fence post socket

Fig. 8

post

cover slides up for access

hole for post

spacing pieces

vertical board covers

metal post socket

PROJECTS

TRICKS WITH TRELLIS

OST TRELLIS tends to be made from small sawn sections about 12 × 18 mm (½ × ¾ in) up to 20 × 34 mm (⅞ × 1¼ in), depending on how stout you wish it to appear. You have the choice of PAR small sections or larger sawn battens, as standard, usually from the woodyard. If you have a large order, they will probably cut to the section you want, and advise what sizes are best value. If you have a sawbench, then you can rip down large sawn boards to suit. Remember that every sawcut puts some of your board in the dust sack.

The amount you see through depends on the gauge – that is to say, how far apart the strips are spaced. It is mainly a matter of taste. The crossings are nailed and the nails clenched on the back. On special pieces, the joints may be halved or partly halved, but this involves a lot of work. Such details are generally found in architectural infill work, with PAR sections of not less than 18 × 18 mm (¾ × ¾ in).

Diagonal trellis is a good structural brace, and will not go out of shape if pressure is applied to a corner. Square trellis involves less cutting work and is easy to set up, once you have decided on the gauge and wood section. The useful jigs shown in Fig. 1 may help to position the strips when nailing.

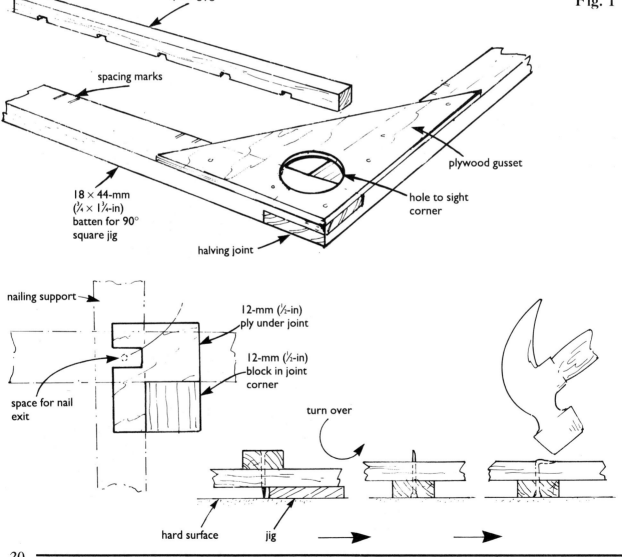

Fig. 1

spacing jig

spacing marks

plywood gusset

18 × 44-mm (¾ × 1¼-in) batten for 90° square jig

hole to sight corner

halving joint

nailing support

12-mm (½-in) ply under joint

12-mm (½-in) block in joint corner

space for nail exit

turn over

hard surface

jig

CURVED TOPS

If the trellis is to top a fence, then the latter will hold it rigid. You can fix a strip of wood in a gentle sweep to its top edge, as in Fig. 2. Avoid sharp curves, or laminate several thin strips together and pre-bend them to fit, as in Fig. 3. You can then trim the vertical strips to length, using this strip as a marking template (Fig. 4).

Where the curved top trellis is not nailed to a fence in order to give it rigidity against the spring of a bent top strip, it will try to curve up in the middle. To avoid this, always laminate and make up the trellis with a

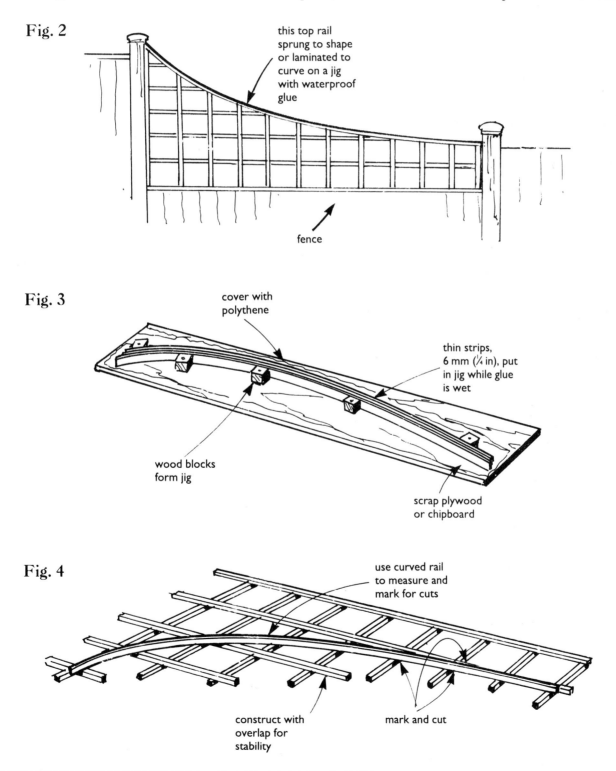

Fig. 2

this top rail
sprung to shape
or laminated to
curve on a jig
with waterproof
glue

fence

Fig. 3

cover with
polythene

thin strips,
6 mm (¼ in), put
in jig while glue
is wet

wood blocks
form jig

scrap plywood
or chipboard

Fig. 4

use curved rail
to measure and
mark for cuts

construct with
overlap for
stability

mark and cut

temporary plank of wood between the bottom horizontal strips to hold it level (Fig. 5).

Small-radius top features, such as that in Fig. 6, are best cut from 6- or 9-mm (¼- or ⅜-in) exterior-grade plywood. Nail these to the top trellis strip and add a capping strip to make up the thickness. This avoids a skimpy appearance in the curved feature, or a mismatch of the thicknesses. The back of

the ply has to be level with the back of the horizontal strips, so that the verticals can go behind and be nailed.

Where both sides of the feature are visible, the spaces between the verticals around the exposed rear face of the ply arch will show. The answer to this one is to add some infill. You can do this with shaped pieces of trellis strip to match the outer curve. It looks better edge-on too.

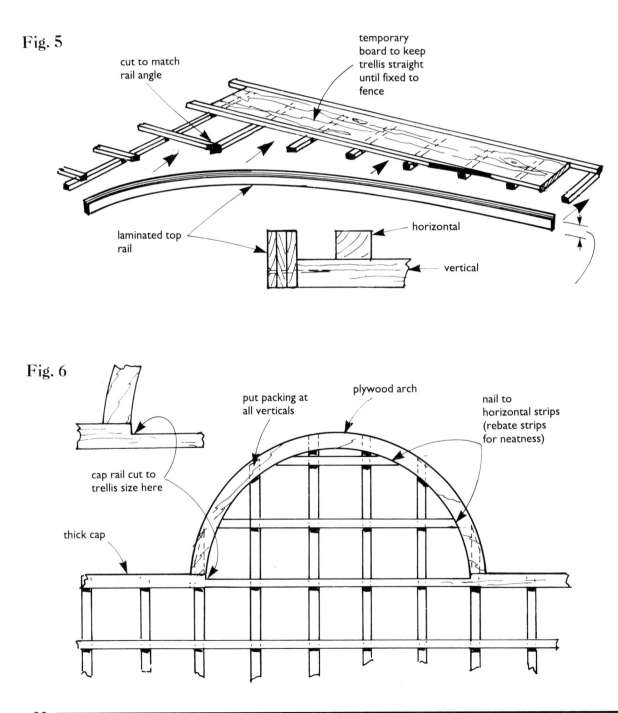

Fig. 5

cut to match rail angle

temporary board to keep trellis straight until fixed to fence

laminated top rail

horizontal

vertical

Fig. 6

put packing at all verticals

plywood arch

nail to horizontal strips (rebate strips for neatness)

cap rail cut to trellis size here

thick cap

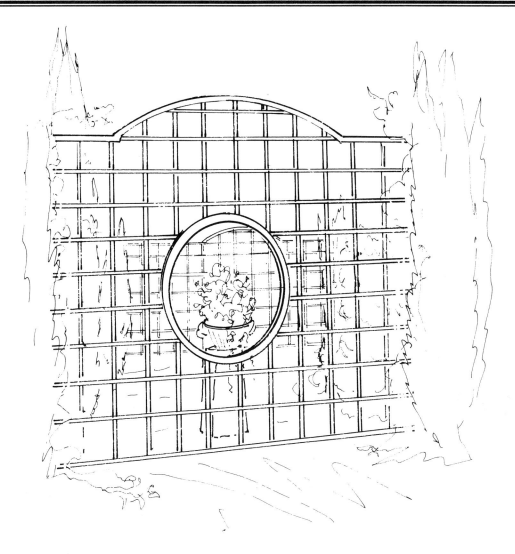

PEEPHOLE TRELLIS

Although overall sizes are given in Fig. 1, the size you choose will depend on your garden site. Try to keep the same proportions, scaling them up or down to suit (within reason). You will then be able to work out a different cutting list.

You can also produce the effect of greater distance in a smaller garden by using a spot of perspective trickery. Study Fig. 2. Suppose the trellis is to be seen most often from a particular vantage point – as a glimpse between trees, for example, or from a patio door. By the simple expedient of producing a reduced-scale version of the first trellis and placing it a comparatively short distance behind the first, you will make the second piece seem much further away than it is. Enhance this effect by

CUTTING LIST				
Section		No.	Length	
mm	in		mm	in
25 × 25	1 × 1	9	2667	105
		6	1880	74
		8	1650	65
51 × 25	2 × 1	2	711	28
4	³/₁₆ ext. ply	1	711	28 dia.
		1	1677 × 230	66 × 9

TOOLS

Cross-cut saw
Tenon saw
Jigsaw
Hammer

Fig. 1

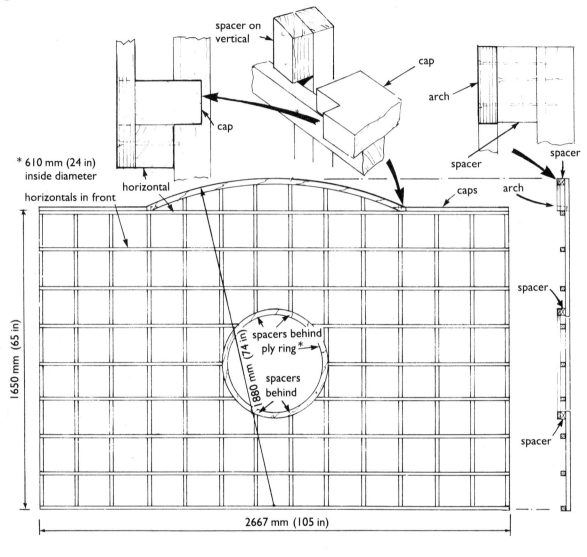

spacer on vertical

cap

cap

arch

spacer

spacer

* 610 mm (24 in) inside diameter

horizontal

horizontals in front

caps

arch

spacer

1650 mm (65 in)

1880 mm (74 in)

spacers behind ply ring *

spacers behind

spacer

spacer

2667 mm (105 in)

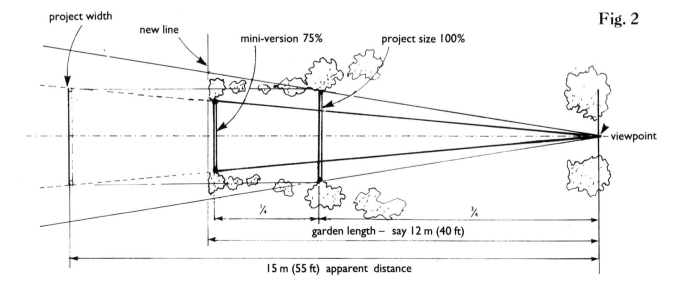

Fig. 2

project width

new line

mini-version 75%

project size 100%

viewpoint

¼

¾

garden length – say 12 m (40 ft)

15 m (55 ft) apparent distance

tapering a path, or planting smaller shrubs near its ends. Take advantage of the second scale on the drawing for this one.

1 Use a piece of wood with pencil and nail to mark circles for the peephole and arcs for the top. Fig. 3 shows a neat way of fitting the shapes on a ply sheet; should you alter the scale of your version, do some checking first.

Cut the shapes with a jigsaw. You may be able to clamp it to the strip of wood that served as a compass, but make sure that the blade is at right angles to the radius, or it will try to run off or run in.

2 Cut enough vertical strips to fit each side of the arch, with the overlength ones towards the centre. Ignore the peephole for now. Cut all the horizontals and, using a jig, nail them to the verticals. Mark the centre and nail on the ply top. Rebate the 51 × 25-mm (2 × 1-in) cap strips to fit each side of this. Remember that the top horizontal strip goes full width, not just across the arch part. This steadies the trellis and maintains lateral stiffness at the top. Do not make the panel longer, or it will be weak. Fit it between posts and add other plain panels on each side.

Lay the ring of ply in position and nail it to the horizontals, then fit short vertical offcut pieces to pack behind the ply where the verticals pass it. Nail and glue these

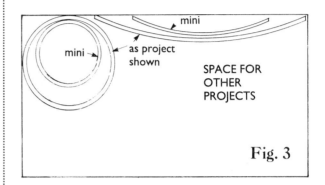

Fig. 3

joints. When set, remove the strips within the ring flush with the inside edge. Do this carefully with a jigsaw or pad saw.

To make the small 'trick version', choose small-section timber in proportion and reduce the spacing, so that there are the same number of strips. Remember to mount it on thinner posts too.

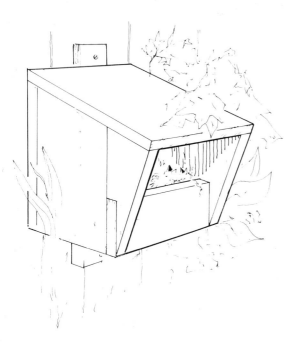

OPEN NEST BOX

Robins are known to nest in quite strange places – old kettles, for example – but to encourage these friendly visitors the wooden box shown here is a firm favourite.

The material is thick, so as to provide insulation from cold spring weather and hot sun when the hatchlings are growing. There are side cheeks to keep out the wind and an overhanging roof to keep it dry. This is the limit for enclosure, as robins do not like the 'hole' type of box. It is a simple 'saw and nail' exercise, one which might encourage young woodworkers to have a go.

Fig. 1 shows the design. Please do not change the main dimensions, which have been chosen to suit the birds' nesting habits, and give the right amount of room for them to build their nests. (They are particular in their choice – even when it's a kettle!)

Sawn wood, with its rough texture, will blend in with the setting, and afford a grip for perching. If you use this grade of wood, dress the rough surface with a light chisel stroke wherever it joins a cut edge. This will prevent water from staying in the joints and will even allow waterproof glue to be used in addition to nails. A nest box, however, is never intended to be given anything more

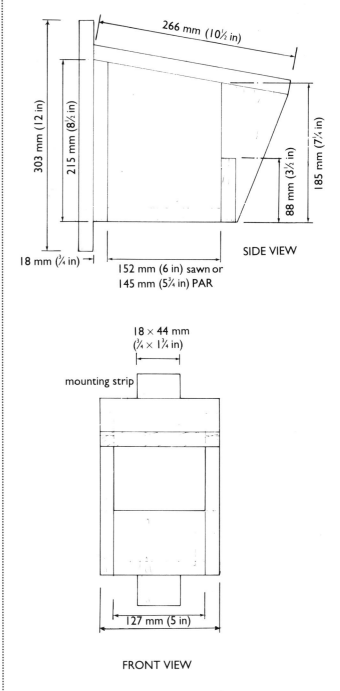

Fig. 1

SIDE VIEW

FRONT VIEW

than a preservative stain finish; the birds do not want to be easily seen by predators.

If you are going to use offcuts of planed wood you can give it a rustic surface that will blend in with the garden and will afford good purchase for the birds' claws. Cut some strips of bark from old wood in the garden, treat the sawn face with preservative and fix the strips of bark to the front of the nest box with thin long panel pins.

1 Mark out the board, allowing double lines to indicate the saw-cut widths, known as 'kerfs'. If this is not done, each part will be undersize. Use the 90-degree square for all cross-markings except those for the roof, where the longitudinal measurements will give the required angle. The remaining small pieces form the floor and side cheeks. These side cheeks will be shaped later; just make a dividing diagonal cut for now. Fig. 2 shows the marking.

2 De-whisker the pieces and check them for match. You will find that the back is a little higher than the side on its front edge. Mark where the sloping side meets it, draw a line between the side marks and chamfer the front corner to match the side slope. This can be done with a chisel, cutting diagonally from the line, all along the front. You will be cutting across the grain, so take it in small, easy stages, pairing the shavings away.

The roof should now sit on the sides as well as the back.

MATERIALS

Sawn pine board, 25 × 150 mm (1 × 6 in), which looks rustic and needs work at the joints, or choose the slightly smaller 18 × 145 mm (¾ × 5¾ in) planed (PAR), referred to in DIY shops as PSE (planed square edge). You will need a piece 1321 mm (52 in) long. This is for the box. You also need a strip of 18 × 44 mm (¾ × 1¾ in), 303 mm (12 in) long, for mounting the box to a fence or post amongst shrubs. An offcut will do.

TOOLS

Cross-cut and tenon saws
Hammer
Screwdriver
Drill
Chisel
Adjustable and fixed carpenter's squares
Marking knife
Rule

Fig. 2

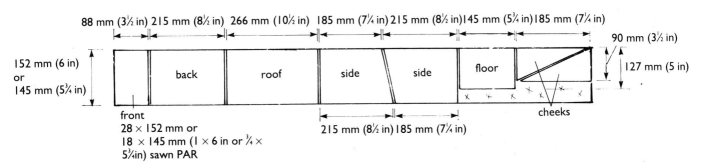

length 1325 mm (52 in)

88 mm (3½ in) 215 mm (8½ in) 266 mm (10½ in) 185 mm (7¼ in) 215 mm (8½ in) 145 mm (5¾ in) 185 mm (7¼ in)

90 mm (3½ in)

152 mm (6 in) or 145 mm (5¾ in)

back   roof   side   side   floor

127 mm (5 in)

cheeks

front
28 × 152 mm or
18 × 145 mm (1 × 6 in or ¾ × 5¾ in) sawn PAR

215 mm (8½ in) 185 mm (7¼ in)

3 Nail and, if desired, glue the box together, remembering to have the chamfered edge of the back facing to the front. Nail the sides to the floor and then add the back. Turn it over and nail on the short front piece. Sit it in its floor and fix the roof. The roof does not need any chamfers, even though it is angled. See Fig. 3.

4 Measure the position of the notches and the angles on the remaining triangular side cheeks (Fig. 4). An easy way of making sure that they will fit is to position them against the sides, the roof and front panel ends, as shown in Fig. 5, when the exact shape can be drawn on. This will take care of any slight variations that may have crept in due to the thicknesses of the available wood. Glue and nail from the roof, and into the top part of the front panel. Avoid nailing through the pointed lower corner, which may split, or pre-drill for a small pin here. In fact, you may find the following method useful wherever nailing or pinning is to be done on fragile areas: first make sure that the joint is closed, to support the wood, then gently press in the panel pin instead of hitting it.

Fig. 3

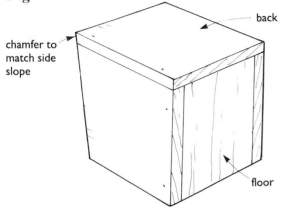

chamfer to match side slope

back

floor

Fig. 4

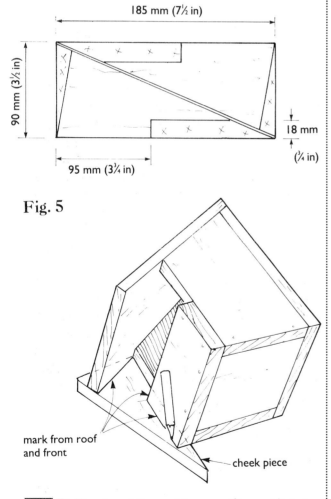

185 mm (7½ in)

90 mm (3½ in)

95 mm (3¾ in)

18 mm (¾ in)

Fig. 5

mark from roof and front

cheek piece

5 Drill the 18 × 44-mm (¾ × 1¾-in) support strip near each end and nail or screw it vertically to the back of the box. Treat the whole item with brown preservative stain. Do not use the water-based variety if the box is made from planed

material, and choose a type which is not harmful to wildlife when dry. Keep the box in the open air so that it will weather and lose any smell. If it is hung up so that the front is downwards, birds will avoid it during this time.

Set it up in its intended position in the winter or after hatching time. It should be low – say 1 to 2 metres (3 to 6 ft) from the ground in a secluded area on a fence, wall or post, with foliage close by. It should not face prevailing cold winds, but it must be shaded from the midday sun.

Patience is needed, even with robins. Never handle the box or get too close when nesting has started. Just before Christmas, clear out the old nest, for next year's building session.

GABLED NEST BOX

This box is intended for smaller birds, such as tits, which prefer access through a hole high up in the box. For this reason the roof has been formed in a gable, although some types with flat or sloping roofs also appeal.

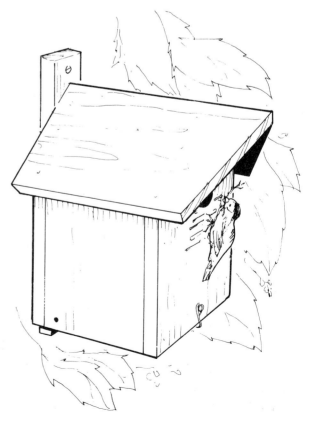

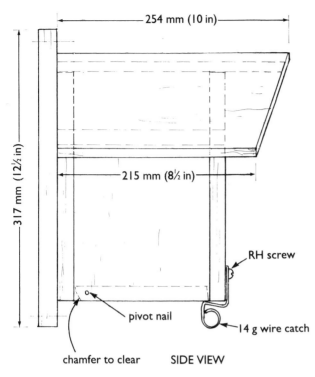

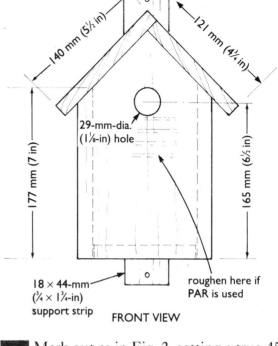

Fig. 1

SIDE VIEW

FRONT VIEW

The gable produces a good internal shape, as nests are built almost up to the hole, to give a deep nesting hollow. The roof overhangs to give secluded entry and weatherproofing. The floor is hinged so that old nests may be cleaned away.

While some boxes are made from planed wood, the front at least should be either from sawn material or scored with a saw or knife to give some claw-purchase near the hole. Some types have a short perch below the hole, but because this may encourage predators, it has been omitted here.

The same tool kit, plus pliers, will do. Add a piece of coathanger wire to the materials list. The box needs slightly more of the same-section wood: 1410 mm (55½ in) and 317 mm (12½ in) respectively. The plans are shown in Fig. 1.

1 Mark out as in Fig. 2, setting a true 45-degree angle on the adjustable square. The dimensions include waste for chamfering the side pieces. If you are not experienced in cutting a 45-degree angle with the aid of a tilting circular saw, it is unlikely that you will be able to chamfer both side pieces in one go. For this reason the marking has been dimensioned to give enough room for two cuts.

2 After cutting the parts, follow Fig. 3 as you mark and cut the chamfers on the top of the sides. Set the marking gauge to the wood thickness, or scribe a line along the edge of a piece of similar thickness, placed vertically on top and flush with the edge. Whatever the thickness of the wood, provided both pieces are the same thickness

Fig. 2

length 1410 mm (55½ in)

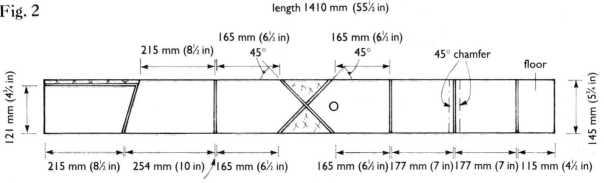

Fig. 3

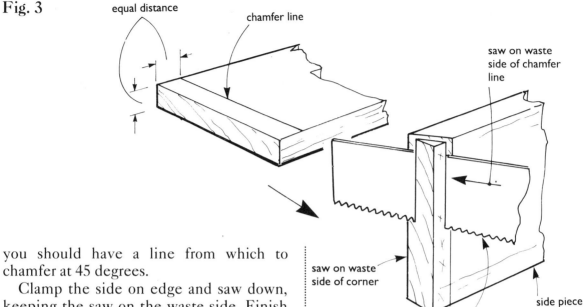

you should have a line from which to chamfer at 45 degrees.

Clamp the side on edge and saw down, keeping the saw on the waste side. Finish off with glasspaper on a block, or use a plane or belt sander (just some of those optional extras that speed things up). Drill the entrance hole with a flat bit and open it out to the exact size. Do not over-enlarge it if you want to attract blue tits.

3 Nail and, if desired, glue the back and front to the sides, so that they overlap flush. Glue and nail one roof panel to its opposite panel, and nail them to the front, back and sides. The floor is then placed loose and free in position.

4 Remove the floor and put a small nail in the underside, so that you can lift it out while checking for easy clearance. The front and back edges will have to be chamfered slightly. Pivot the floor on small nails through pre-drilled holes in the sides. The fit does not have to be tight. Bend a wire clip with pliers and screw it to the front so that it springs back to secure the floor.

5 Nail or screw the mounting strip vertically to the back after applying preservative to the outside only. Mount the box on a fence or wall amongst close bushes at least 2 metres (6 ft) high.

Alternatively, choose a tree site, provided it is secluded and faces the right way. Do not nail or screw directly to the tree trunk, for as the tree grows, it will be damaged. Metal or

wire straps have the same effect after some years. However, a piece of plastic-covered spring curtain wire will stretch to accommodate tree growth. Fig. 4 shows the method. First, run some oil into the hollow spring wire, to prevent rust. Fit the hooks at each end and provide matching screws in the box sides. If you use this method, the box does not need the mounting strip.

Fig. 4

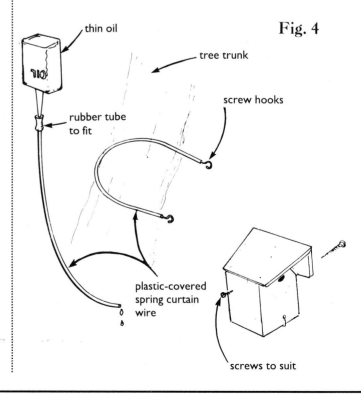

BIRD FEEDER

This can be hung from a tree branch. The whole assembly is shown in Fig. 1.

1 With drill and chisel, cut a hole in the centre of the square plywood to take the central post. Chamfer the long edge of the other two pieces of plywood to meet at 15 degrees, then notch these faces to fit halfway round the post.

2 Form rebates in four of the 18 × 18-mm (¾ × ¾-in) strips to take the square ply. They have to be deep to leave an overhang or 'drip' to shed the rain. Mitre the corners and check that they fit all round the ply. Glue these up and add a few panel pins.

3 Chamfer the ends of two more strips and screw them to the post each side of the hole. Check with a try square for 90 degrees to this. They will support the ply floor.

Saw two pieces of 18 × 44 mm (¾ × 1¾-in) to form 15-degree roof supports, notch them to fit round the remaining 18 × 18-mm (¾-in) strip, upon which you now form a double chamfer. Cut this to form two ridge pieces.

4 Glue and screw the supports and ridge to the post and fit the roof. Check the height and angles.

5 Sand, drill for a hanging cord and treat with preservative.

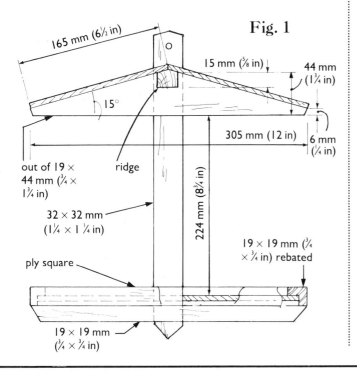

Fig. 1

165 mm (6½ in)

15 mm (⅝ in)

44 mm (1¾ in)

15°

305 mm (12 in)

6 mm (¼ in)

out of 19 × 44 mm (¾ × 1¾ in)

ridge

32 × 32 mm (1¼ × 1¼ in)

224 mm (8¾ in)

19 × 19 mm (¾ × ¾ in) rebated

ply square

19 × 19 mm (¾ × ¾ in)

CUTTING LIST

Section		No.	Length	
mm	in		mm	in
18 × 18	¾ × ¾	7	318	12½
18 × 44	¾ × 1¾	2	318	12½
32 × 32	1¼	1	343	13½
4	⅙ ext. ply	1	304 × 305	12 × 12
		2	304 × 165	12 × 6½

TOOLS

Cross-cut and tenon saws
Chisels
Drill
Screwdriver
Hammer
Rebate plane or router

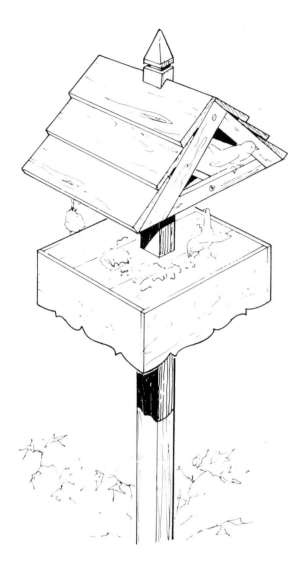

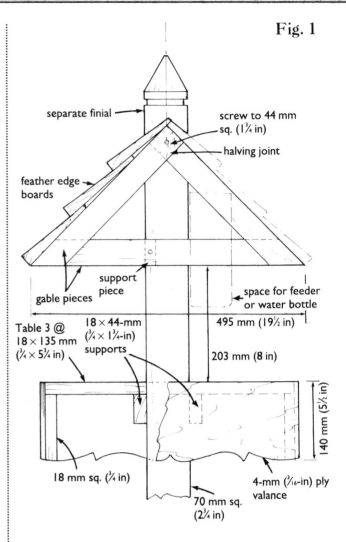

Fig. 1

separate finial

screw to 44 mm sq. (1¾ in)

halving joint

feather edge boards

support piece

gable pieces

space for feeder or water bottle

Table 3 @ 18 × 135 mm (¾ × 5¾ in)

18 × 44-mm (¾ × 1¾-in) supports

495 mm (19½ in)

203 mm (8 in)

140 mm (5½ in)

18 mm sq. (¾ in)

70 mm sq. (2¾ in)

4-mm (³⁄₁₆-in) ply valance

WHILE NEST BOXES are functional, their shape dictated by practicalities, feeding tables can be decorative as well as providing shelter from the rain, which might wash away food. Hopefully, predators will be deterred from climbing up and around the valance that surrounds the table. The post can be placed in a pre-sunk hole, or bolted to a replaceable short stub post, or clamped to a metal-post-repair spike, as described earlier (see page 18). Site the table in good view but fairly close to a hedge, trees or bushes, where the birds may hide if disturbed.

Fig. 1 shows the arrangement, which requires a certain sequence of assembly for easy construction.

The roof gable ends are made with halving joints. Mark one cutting line by scribing along the edge of the next while it is held in position. Clamp the wood upright in a vice or Workmate and, using a tenon saw, cut down on the waste side of central with the grain. Then saw cross-grain to free the waste. If the cross-grain cut is made *first*, the saw may go too deep. This will weaken the joint, whereas an over-deep cut *with* the grain will not damage so many fibres.

Mark and cut the second piece, using the first rebate to set the depth (which should have been finished on the centre line). Do the 90-degree top joint first, then clamp it and mark the 45-degree pairs. Remember that one angled strip will have two halving rebates on one face and the other will have one on each. Remember this when gluing up. See Fig. 2, which also shows how the roof is fitted to the post.

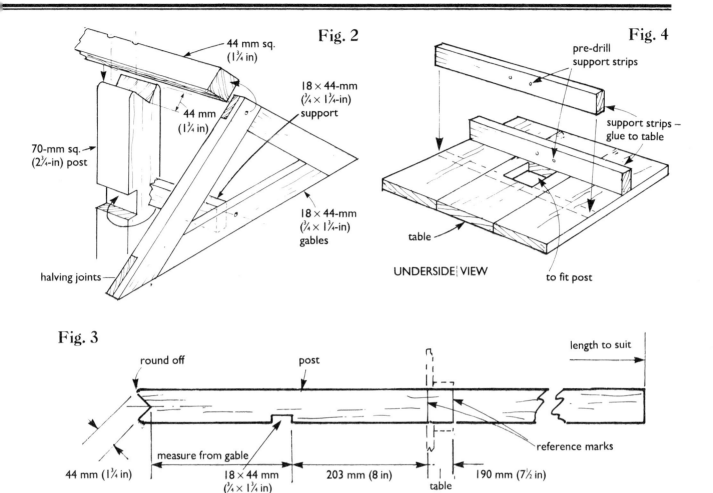

Fig. 2

44 mm sq. (1¾ in)

44 mm (1¾ in)

70-mm sq. (2¾-in) post

18 × 44-mm (¾ × 1¾-in) support

18 × 44-mm (¾ × 1¾-in) gables

halving joints

Fig. 4

pre-drill support strips

support strips – glue to table

table

UNDERSIDE VIEW

to fit post

Fig. 3

round off

post

length to suit

measure from gable

44 mm (1¾ in)

18 × 44 mm (¾ × 1¾ in)

203 mm (8 in)

table

190 mm (7½ in)

reference marks

2 Cut the post to length – it should be about 1.5 to 2 metres (5 to 6 ft) high, plus any that goes below ground. If the post does go below the ground, remember that it must be dropped into a hole that has already been made; the finished piece of woodwork cannot be hammered in, for it might be damaged.

Cut a 'V' notch in the top and a rebate to take a cross-support for the roof ends, as in Fig. 3. Mark the position of the table supports below.

3 Cut three strips of 18 × 145 mm (¾ × 5¾ in) for the table. Make a square hole with drill and jigsaw, or pad saw, in the centre of one piece. Edge-glue the others each side and pre-drill two 18 × 44-mm (¾ × 1¾-in) battens, as shown in Fig. 4. Glue, nail or screw the boards to them, so that they are flush outside the hole, again as in Fig. 4. Remember that these strips will be underneath.

4 Slide the table part on to the post until the upper mark meets the table-top. Use a square to set it at right angles to the post and pierce through the screw holes to mark their position on the post. Slide the table up a little and pilot-drill the post for four screws.

Return the table to its marks and screw the battens to the post, checking again with the square in both directions (Fig. 5).

Fig. 5

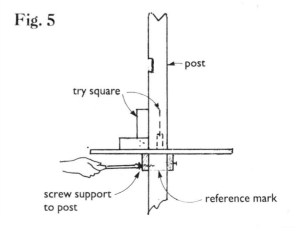

post

try square

screw support to post

reference mark

CUTTING LIST				
Section		**No.**	**Length**	
mm	in		mm	in
70 × 70	2¾ × 2¾		2130 (plus extra if it is set in the ground)	84
18 × 145	¾ × 5¾	3	457	18
44 × 44	1¾ × 1¾	1	457	18
18 × 44	¾ × 1¾	4	381	15
		2	508	20
		3	457	18
18 × 18	¾ × ¾	4	114	4½
6	¼ ext. ply	4	470 × 140	18½ × 5½
Feather edge 150 (this one is sawn material)	6	6	457	18

TOOLS

Cross-cut, tenon and coping saws
Chisels
Hand-drill
Screwdrivers
Hammer
Router (optional)
Jigsaw (optional)

5 Cut four rectangles of exterior-grade plywood 6 mm (¼ in) thick. These are to form the valance. Clamp them together and cut the decorative curves to the lower edge in one block with a jigsaw, or coping saw, as in Fig. 6. Each will overlap the next

Fig. 6

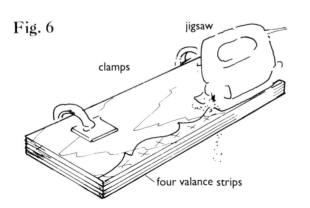

four valance strips
jigsaw
clamps

at one end, so all are identical. Mark the inner face of each one to avoid using any 'back to front'. Clean up the edges with glasspaper.

6 Glue and pin a strip of 18 × 18 mm (¾ × ¾ in) flush behind one end of each valance piece; repeat for all of them (Fig. 7). The short end will fit under the table. Glue and pin the valance pieces to the edge of the table, as in Fig. 8, and secure each to the next corner strip with small screws.

Fig. 7

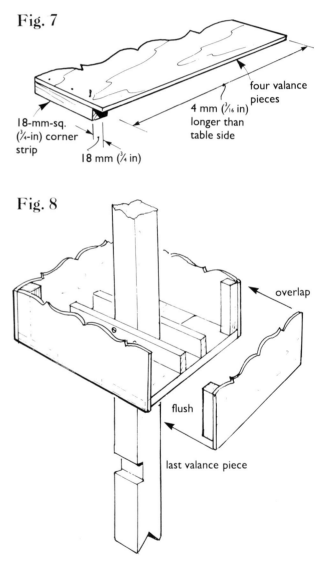

four valance pieces
4 mm (³⁄₁₆ in) longer than table side
18-mm-sq. (¾-in) corner strip
18 mm (¾ in)

Fig. 8

overlap
flush
last valance piece

You may wish to fit the valance so that it projects 6 mm (1¼ in) above the surface of the table. This will prevent crumbs being washed or blown off, but it will also make cleaning difficult.

7 With the table part completed, screw the wood for the roof ridge, 44 × 44 mm (1¾ × 1¾ in), and the cross-support below it, as in Fig. 9. You can now support the post in an upright position while you make the roof.

Fig. 9

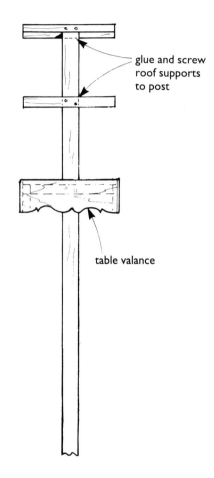

glue and screw roof supports to post

table valance

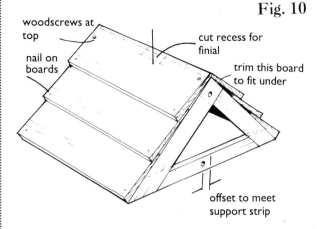

Fig. 10

woodscrews at top

nail on boards

cut recess for finial

trim this board to fit under

offset to meet support strip

9 Follow the marking and cutting sequence in Fig. 11 to make the finial from 70 × 70-mm (2¾ × 2¾-in) post material. Clamp it in a vice while shaping with a tenon saw. Finally, form the 'V' notch to fit the roof. This will not be exactly 45 degrees, because the roof boards taper, so mark the angles by scribing directly from the end of the roof itself.

Fig. 11

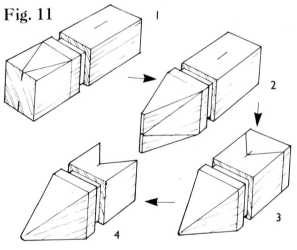

8 Cut six pieces of feather-edged board and nail them to the end gable frames, as in Fig. 10. Remember to use small woodscrews in pre-drilled holes in the topmost corners of the top board, which might split if nailed.

Drill both gables to take screws which will fix them to the ends of the top and lower cross-pieces already on the post. Note that the lower holes are offset, to match the position of the lower strip. Screw it in place and mark the ridge to match the post, ready for a finial. Having reached this point in the proceedings, do not be tempted to bang the thing into the ground. It is not so designed.

10 Clean up the sawn finish of the roof, and apply preservative stain. Allow this to dry and weather thoroughly before supplying any food. Seed- and nut-feeders and a water hopper can be mounted under the roof. Do not hang feeders below the valance, which is there to prevent the access of predators or squirrels, who also like nuts.

Clean the table-top periodically to remove stale food and droppings. Use soap and water for cleaning – if you scrape the table-top dry, the preservative will wear away.

PLANTER PAIR

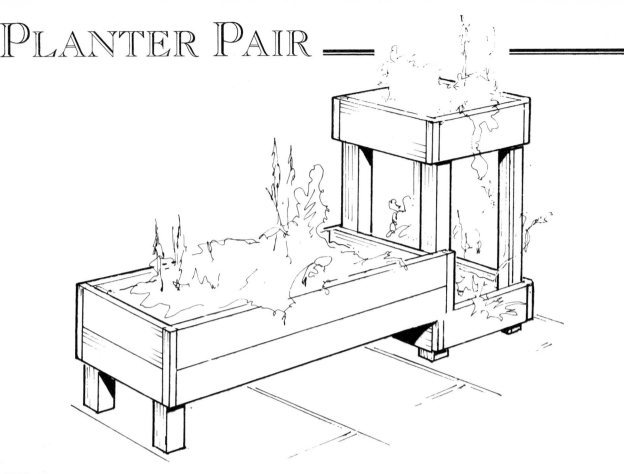

PLANTERS come in various shapes and sizes. Success in arranging groups of them in an artistic manner depends on how they match in style and contrast in size.

Not only is this design a group in itself, but it shows a different outline when seen from different viewpoints. This gives added interest, and allows you to experiment with combinations of flowers and miniature shrubs in a range of sizes.

While you are waiting for bulbs to pop through, there is an optional slatted seat for the largest container (Fig. 1). This will also serve as a windbreak, backdrop or support for taller plants (Fig. 2). When its bottom is lifted out, the lowest of the containers can be used to enclose pots resting on the ground (Fig. 3).

When two or more units are made, the possibilities increase enormously. Take two, for example. From the basic side view in Fig. 4, a rhythmic run will lock together (Fig. 5). Put them end to end, as in Fig. 6, and you have a frame for a view or an enclosure for a wall-hung feature. Try them back to back for a central block (Fig. 7) or in a corner. And how about end to end as in Fig. 8, to frame a shrub in an ordinary round tub? Try them stepped from a raised patio, near a wall or steps, as shown in Fig. 9. In

Fig. 1

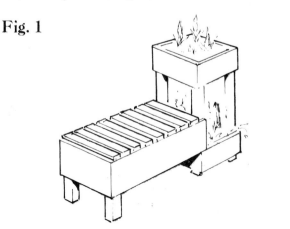

Fig. 2

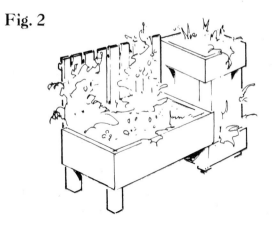

Fig. 3

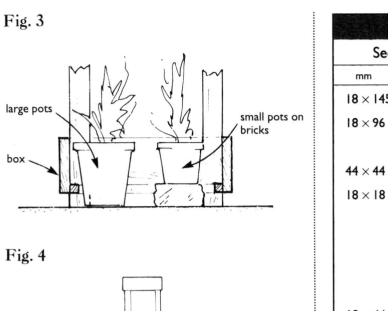

- large pots
- box
- small pots on bricks

Fig. 4

Fig. 5

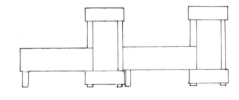

Fig. 6

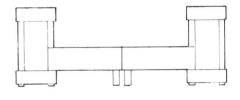

Fig. 7

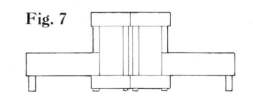

Fig. 8

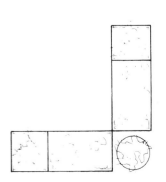

Fig. 9

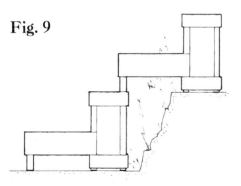

CUTTING LIST

Section		No.	Length	
mm	in		mm	in
18 × 145	3/4 × 5 3/4	10	406	16
18 × 96	3/4 × 3 3/4	4	711	28
		4	406	16
44 × 44	1 3/4 × 1 3/4	4	761	30
18 × 18	3/4 × 3/4*	2	667	26 1/4
		2	673	26 1/2
		4	180	7 3/4
		10	318	12 1/2
		8	145	5 3/4
18 × 44	3/4 × 1 3/4*	9	406	16
4	3/16 ext. ply	1	406 × 673	16 × 26 1/2
		2	406 × 406	16 × 16

* Optional seat parts

TOOLS

Saw
Drill and drill bits
Screwdriver
Hammer
Carpenter's square

Fig. 10

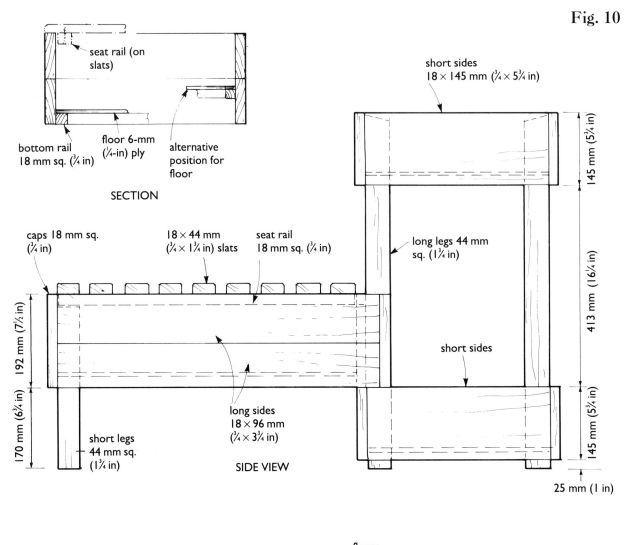

seat rail (on slats)

bottom rail
18 mm sq. (¾ in)

floor 6-mm
(¼-in) ply

alternative
position for
floor

SECTION

short sides
18 × 145 mm (¾ × 5¾ in)

145 mm (5¾ in)

long legs 44 mm
sq. (1¾ in)

413 mm (16¼ in)

short sides

145 mm (5¾ in)

25 mm (1 in)

caps 18 mm sq.
(¾ in)

18 × 44 mm
(¾ × 1¾ in) slats

seat rail
18 mm sq. (¾ in)

192 mm (7½ in)

170 mm (6¾ in)

short legs
44 mm sq.
(1¾ in)

long sides
18 × 96 mm
(¾ × 3¾ in)

SIDE VIEW

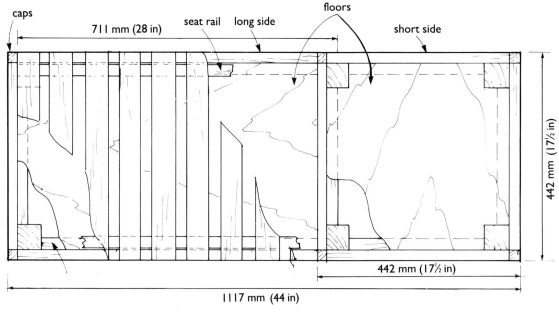

caps

711 mm (28 in)

seat rail   long side

floors

short side

442 mm (17½ in)

442 mm (17½ in)

1117 mm (44 in)

TOP VIEW

this case, though, the lower one must be well ballasted with soil, and firmly supported on solid paving or secured to a wall, so that the upper one does not tip over.

The most simple of glued and screwed joints make this a good early project. The prototype has been made from PAR, because I suggest that you paint it in keeping with the house. The smooth surface of the wood facilitates easy gluing and clamping with woodscrews. Fig. 10 shows the main dimensions. You can enlarge the overall length and width (and perhaps the height a little).

The basic sides fit flush with the corners of the legs, so that alignment is easy. This means that two sets of end grain would be exposed. Cap strips improve the finish and protect the wood. The bottoms of the boxes are 6-mm (¼-in) exterior-grade plywood and may be made removable if required.

The optional seat is a row of slats screwed and glued to small-section rails. It should *not* be used as a bridge seat between end supports. Each slat rests on the edge of the box. The general cutaway in Fig. 11 shows the corner detail from inside.

Note that some of the box bottoms may be raised a little, so that you can use shallow, more economical planting or small pots.

Fig. 11

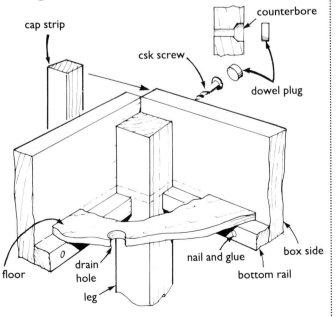

cap strip

counterbore

csk screw

dowel plug

floor

drain hole

leg

nail and glue

bottom rail

box side

0

1 Mark the lengths of each side on the planks. Make double lines to allow for the sawcut or 'kerf'. If this is not done, each piece will be shorter than intended. Use a carpenter's square for true 90-degree cutting lines.

Do the same for each of the remaining pieces for the whole project. Keep each batch together and write the part name on each set. Mark right round the leg material, so that the sawcuts may be truly square in both directions.

Use the actual boards to measure the lengths of the cap strips, as some woodyard or DIY finished sizes may be fractionally different from the drawings.

2 Saw the parts to length with a cross-cut handsaw or hand-held circular saw. Support the wood firmly with a minimum of overhang, so that it does not vibrate or skew. Ease off the sawing pressure as the cut is completed to avoid splitting the last corner. Stack the sets of small strips together.

3 Remove any whiskers with a light stroke of glasspaper, then find a flat surface on which to lay out the parts in position. Mark each joint with an identity number or letter on both pieces. This will ensure that it, and any holes, match up.

Drill where screws are to go, making a 3-mm (⅛-in) pilot hole through the board and into the leg, while they are in position. Then, with the board on a scrap piece of wood to protect the drill bit, enlarge to take the screws clear. Now counter-bore 6 mm (¼ in) deep to accommodate the screwhead itself. This recess will be plugged later with dowel slices. At this stage work on only four of the short sides in the 18 × 145 mm (¾ × 5¾ in) and the long legs. This sub-assembly will be part of the tall element of this project.

WATCHPOINT

Do not drill into a wet glued joint: epoxy is difficult to get off the drill bit!

4 Mix some weatherproof glue (epoxy or polyester). Lay the long legs down and glue the end pieces in place, as in Fig. 12. Use the carpenter's square to align, and make sure that the ends of the boards are flush with the outer edge of each leg. The screws will probably tell you if the identity numbers are mismatched! Tighten the screws to clamp the joint. This assembly is the long end.

Fig. 12

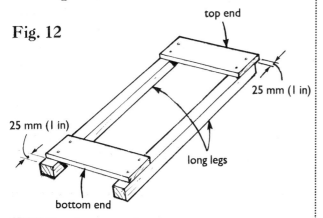

5 Do the same for the other long legs, but add the inner end boards for the large box, as in Fig. 13. One cap strip can be fixed as a guide for a long side later. The other will get in the way. Do not forget that the boards are to be edge-glued just prior to screwing them in place.

Fig. 13

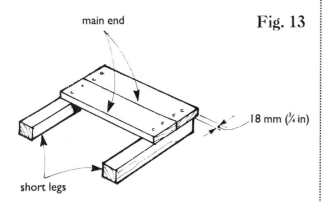

6 Edge-glue the pairs of long boards together. Clamp them with sash or wedge clamps, making sure that the ends are level.

Join the short legs with the remaining pair of end boards, edge-gluing and screwing as before. This is the outer end of the main box (see Fig. 14).

Fig. 14

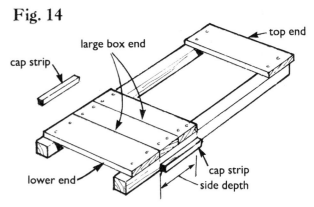

7 You now have some parts with which to check measurements, so mark out the two square ply bottoms to fit the width of the Step 4 and 5 assemblies. Draw round the legs to mark notches at the corners. Both bottoms are shown in Fig. 15.

Fig. 15

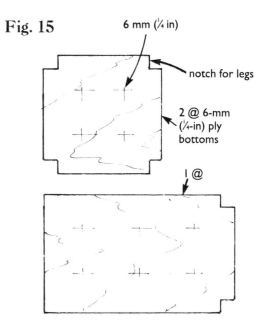

Take both long assemblies and tack them to one ply bottom for alignment. Lay the top and bottom side pieces across and drill for the screws as in Step 3. Make sure that the holes do not clash with those screws already in place. Mix up a small new batch of glue and carry on as before (Fig. 16).

Turn the assembly over and repeat the procedure to complete the tall unit. Add the free cap strip. Both these strips will have to butt close to the long side, so check the latter.

Fig. 16

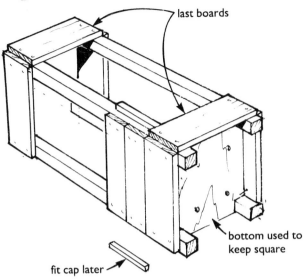

last boards

bottom used to
keep square

fit cap later

8 The main box end will support the now-glued-up sides while butting them up to the cap strips fitted in Step 5. It is even more important to use a square to check for a 90-degree joint here. You can also place a long strip of wood from leg to leg. All should touch.

9 When the glue has set, turn the whole unit over and work on the remaining side. Remember that only a small amount of glue will be needed, but the remaining small sides still have to be fitted to complete the framework.

10 Glue and pin (with nails) the bottom rails flush with the bottom inside edges of all the sides. These will support the bottoms. It is not important if they do not quite meet the legs, provided a dab of glue weatherproofs the end grain.

Cut and try for fit the larger ply bottom, not forgetting the drainage holes, which could do with a lick of epoxy or similar glue on their edges.

11 Glue and pin the cap strips in place at all the corners, and glue in slices of dowel to cap the screw heads. When set, sand off any surplus. Sand the rough edges and corners of the boxes to prevent splitting in use.

THE SEAT

12 Mark the inside width of the box on the slats. Position the 18×18-mm ($\frac{3}{4} \times \frac{3}{4}$-in) rails just inside this and flush with the inside ends of the box. The rails will sit in the recess, over the end legs. Glue and screw the 18×44-mm ($\frac{3}{4} \times 1\frac{3}{4}$-in) slats from rail to slat, so that the screws do not show. Remember to use a square for alignment. Use preservative stain on the seat, as a contrast to the painted outside of the boxes. The insides and bottoms of the boxes should be treated with a plant-safe preservative such as Cuprinol. Water-based preservatives are not recommended for any planed wood.

This is quite a heavy item when filled with soil, so position it before filling or partly empty it before resiting it. Whem moving it empty, keep the removable bottoms in place, so that the joints are not strained.

TIP

The Planter Pair may be a candidate for a proper paint job.

You bought the wood as planed, removed end grain whiskers and rounded things off. In this state, it is not ready for painting. Through working and drying the surface will not be quite as good as before. There will be little uneven areas where you sanded parts to blend in at joints, traces of excess glue and protrusions where screw heads were plugged. Tiny imperfections may not show now, but when the paint is on they will be very obvious.

Sand thoroughly with a flat base sander, such as a belt-type with fine grade or, more slowly with an orbital sander. Fig. 17 shows a greatly enlarged section of the finish as it should be.

Fig. 17

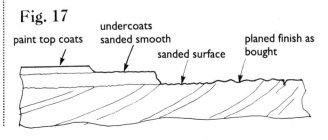

paint top coats

undercoats
sanded smooth

sanded surface

planed finish as
bought

Picnic Bench

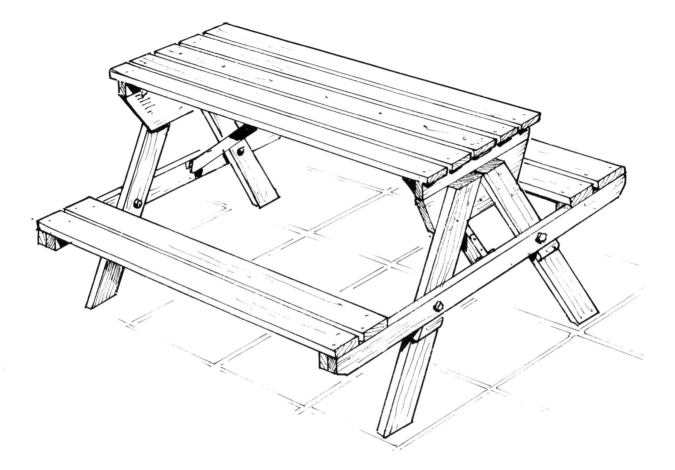

THIS POPULAR ITEM has been designed to be folded up and stored flat, under cover, for the winter. It requires just four bolts and two split pins for reassembly. All the joints are simple, and use weatherproof glue and screws. The general arrangement is shown in Fig. 1.

As you can see from Fig. 1, the seat part is bolted on in one piece and, when stored, fits around the table-top when the legs have been folded inwards. Diagonal struts hold it rigid when assembled.

TOOLS

Cross-cut and tenon saws
Chisels
Drill
Screwdriver
Spanner

CUTTING LIST

Section		No.	Length	
mm	in		mm	in
18 × 44	³/₄ × 1³/₄	1	940	37
		2	610	24
		2	432	17
		4	303 for cutting	12
18 × 69	³/₄ × 2³/₄	4	584	23
18 × 69	³/₄ × 2³/₄	7	1016	40
18 × 95	³/₄ × 3³/₄	4	1066	42
18 × 145	³/₄ × 5³/₄	2	431	17

2 pairs of steel 51-mm (2-in) butts

1 pair of steel 37-mm (1¹/₂-in) back flaps

4 off 51 × 7-mm (2 × ⁵/₁₆-in) steel bolts and nuts with washers

Fig. 1

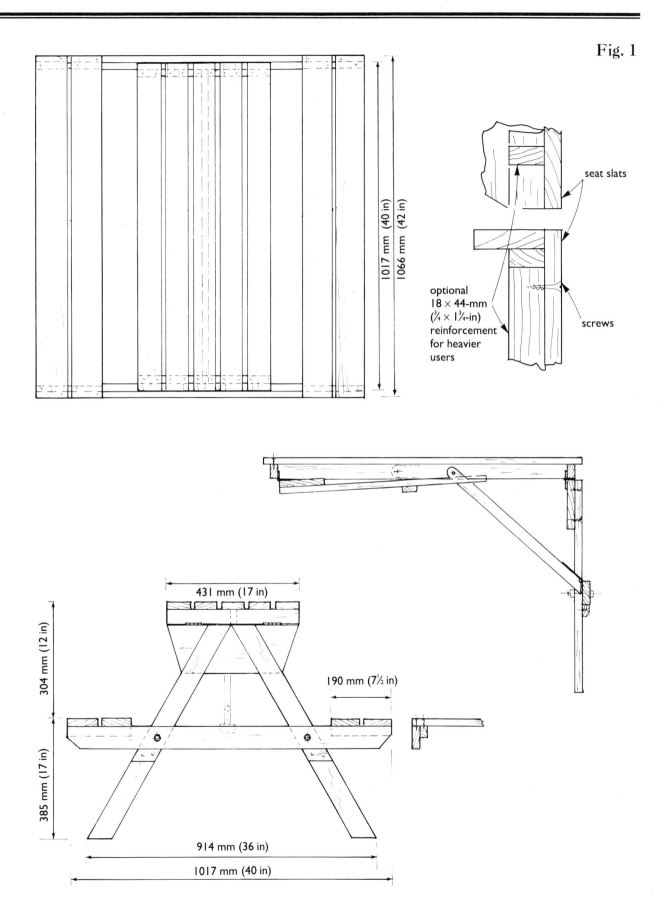

1017 mm (40 in)
1066 mm (42 in)

seat slats

optional
18 × 44-mm
(¾ × 1¾-in)
reinforcement
for heavier
users

screws

431 mm (17 in)

304 mm (12 in)

190 mm (7½ in)

385 mm (17 in)

914 mm (36 in)

1017 mm (40 in)

1 Using a tenon saw and chisel or router, form shallow locating recesses for the legs in two pieces of 18 × 145 mm (¾ × 5¾ in) (see Fig. 2). Mark them out using the 69-mm-wide (2¾-in) leg material set out on the floor to the angle or spread shown in Fig. 1. The recesses must be smooth and level but only 3 mm (⅛ in) deep, to retain strength in these important joining plates.

2 Cut the legs to the correct angle at each end and mark the position for blocks to be glued and screwed on, to take some of the weight imposed by the seats and occupants. Remember to make two each, left- and right-handed. Glue and screw plates to the legs. The legs are outside and the blocks face outwards (see Fig. 3).

3 Make up a pair of similar struts from 18 × 44 mm (¾ × 1¾ in) with scrap 18 × 18 mm (¾ × ¾ in) to thicken them at one end, then drill at the other, rounded, end. Back flaps will be fitted to the thick end of each (Fig. 4).

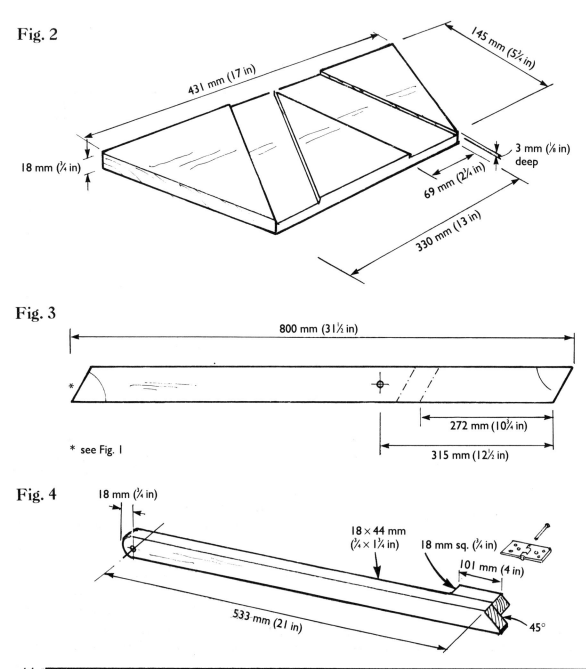

Fig. 2

431 mm (17 in)

145 mm (5¾ in)

18 mm (¾ in)

3 mm (⅛ in) deep

69 mm (2¾ in)

330 mm (13 in)

Fig. 3

800 mm (31½ in)

* see Fig. 1

272 mm (10¾ in)

315 mm (12½ in)

Fig. 4

18 mm (¾ in)

18 × 44 mm (¾ × 1¾ in)

18 mm sq. (¾ in)

101 mm (4 in)

533 mm (21 in)

45°

4 Cut to length, drill and chamfer two seat joiners (Fig. 5). Check that they align with the leg blocks and drill through to clear the 7-mm (⁵⁄₁₆-in) bolts, right through each leg.

5 Form housings in 18 × 69 mm (¾ × 2¾ in) for rebated ends of the table centre rail, which is the same material (Fig. 6). These three pieces form the table-top frame. Glue and screw them together from the ends, using chipboard screws for a better grip.

6 Cut all the table-top slats and seats to their respective lengths. Glue and screw the top slats to the top frame, and two short bearers to the seat joiners. Now glue and screw the seat slats to both these and the joiners. Pivot the struts to the centre rail with 5-mm (³⁄₁₆-in) bolts and nuts or No. 12 screws.

7 Hinge the leg plates to the top end rails so that the legs fold inwards. File off the end of each of the back-flap hinge pins, then drive or drill them out to form four

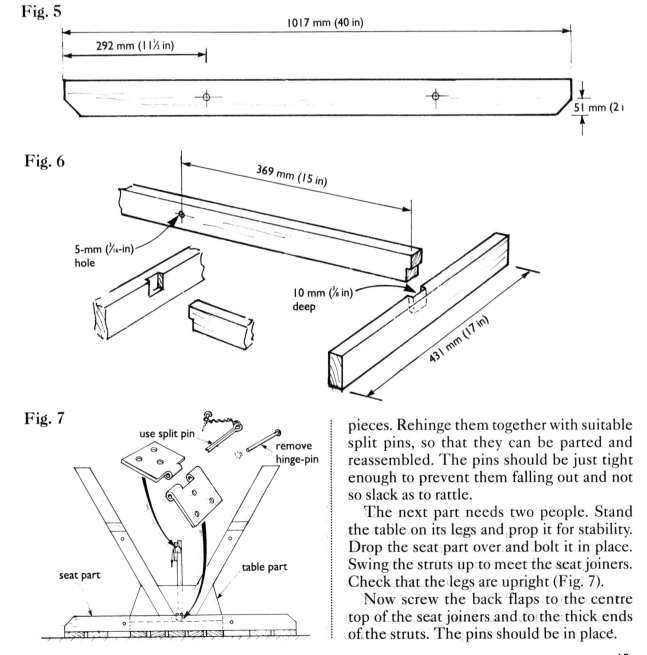

Fig. 5

1017 mm (40 in)

292 mm (11½ in)

51 mm (2 i

Fig. 6

369 mm (15 in)

5-mm (³⁄₁₆-in) hole

10 mm (⅜ in) deep

431 mm (17 in)

Fig. 7

use split pin

remove hinge-pin

seat part

table part

pieces. Rehinge them together with suitable split pins, so that they can be parted and reassembled. The pins should be just tight enough to prevent them falling out and not so slack as to rattle.

The next part needs two people. Stand the table on its legs and prop it for stability. Drop the seat part over and bolt it in place. Swing the struts up to meet the seat joiners. Check that the legs are upright (Fig. 7).

Now screw the back flaps to the centre top of the seat joiners and to the thick ends of the struts. The pins should be in place.

MANY FENCES are available as prefabricated components, but a few basic principles may be helpful in case you need to build a fence or gate to suit a particular site that does not lend itself to the standard treatment. Obviously, there can be no specific cutting lists; it is simply a matter of sketching out your own sizes and applying the ideas shown here.

BOARDED FENCES

Starting at the bottom, there is a horizontal plank in contact with the ground. Horizontal? Well, following the ground line. This is the 'gravel board', which is fixed to the outside face of the posts and sometimes kept upright by a central short peg on the owner's side. All supports face that way.

About 400 mm (16 in) above that is an 'arris rail'. This supports the boards. There is another the same distance from the top edge, and sometimes a central one. These are often triangular in section, cut diagonally from 80 × 80-mm (3 × 3-in) timber. The cut edge is the widest and is placed next to the boards. Each end of the rail is carved to form a rough tenon, set back from the wide face. These fit mortises in the fence posts, which are about 2 to 3 metres (6 to 9 ft) apart, and 150 mm (6 in) square, set in concrete. The vertical boards are feather-edge type, overlapped slightly, resting on the top edge of the gravel board. They continue right across the posts to present a plain face outside. The basic construction is shown in Fig. 1.

Fig. 1

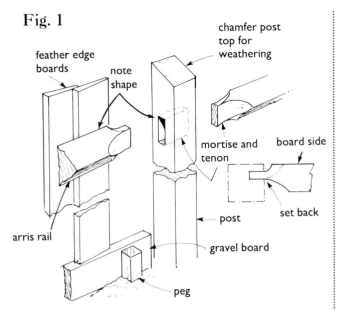

feather edge boards

note shape

chamfer post top for weathering

mortise and tenon

board side

arris rail

post

gravel board

set back

peg

Where the ground slopes gently, the posts remain upright but the arris rails slope, and their tenons are skewed or made loose enough to fit at an angle. The boards are also vertical, but need to be cut to fit the gravel board and then, when all are in place, sawn across in a straight line. Remember that the rails will be longer than those on a level fence, because of the angle; if the timber is of a limited length, the posts may need to be closer. Fig. 2 explains.

Fig. 2

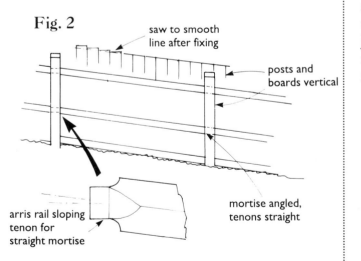

saw to smooth line after fixing

posts and boards vertical

arris rail sloping tenon for straight mortise

mortise angled, tenons straight

When the slope is steep, or changes direction, it is wiser to have the arris rails level and cut extra mortises for them. The boards are still vertical, and need to be progressively longer as they go down the slope. The posts have to be tall enough to take the staggered rails. When the boards

are in place, the top edge still needs to be cut to a neat line, but you have the opportunity of taking it in a pleasing curve to meet the next section of rails, as in Fig. 3.

Fig. 3

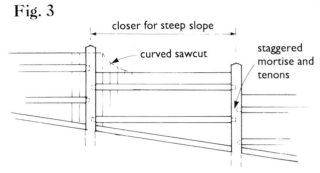

closer for steep slope

curved sawcut

staggered mortise and tenons

INDIVIDUAL BOARD TREATMENT

When privacy is not the main concern, plain vertical boards or battens may be used, to allow ventilation. They could also be arranged at 45-degree angles, either all running parallel or in opposition in alternate panels. For traditional fences, tall or short, any of the examples in Fig. 4 may appeal to you. The pierced, rounded tops and the pointed types are easy to cut with a jigsaw and a curve template or radius-arm attachment, plus a flat-bit drill. The pointed types are straight-sawn in a slot and notch jig, with either a jigsaw or a handsaw, but never a circular saw (which will spoil the 'V' notch).

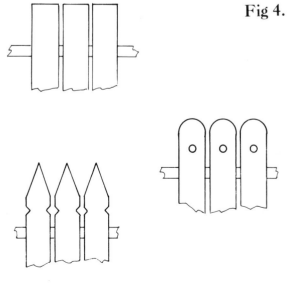

Fig 4.

TALL GATE

This tall garden gate is designed to be set in a close boarded or slightly gapped fence, upswept to meet it. The gate gives privacy, for the gaps are only 12 mm (½ in) wide, and can be closed if you cut the boards from wider material and rebate them with a router, to produce a blind slot, as in Fig. 1, which details the gate and a suitable arch frame. Screw the boards to two cross-rails, and add a brace to resist the tendency to droop from the hinge side. House the strut in specially shaped rebates in the rails. The more force applied by the weight of the gate, the tighter the strut grips the rails. The hinges must be on the edge where the strut meets the lower rail.

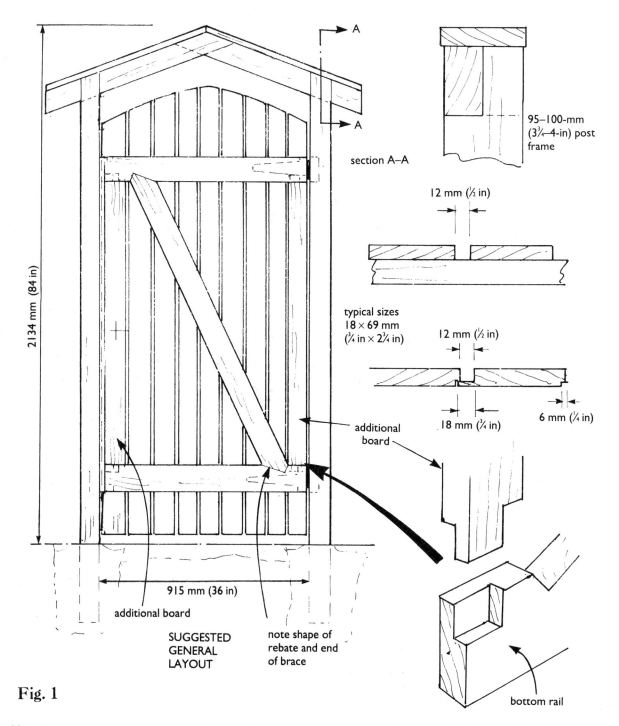

section A–A

95–100-mm (3¾–4-in) post frame

12 mm (½ in)

typical sizes
18 × 69 mm
(¾ in × 2¾ in)

12 mm (½ in)

18 mm (¾ in)

6 mm (¼ in)

additional board

additional board

2134 mm (84 in)

915 mm (36 in)

SUGGESTED GENERAL LAYOUT

note shape of rebate and end of brace

bottom rail

Fig. 1

Above: This view of the Peephole Trellis illustrates how a small hanging basket may be suspended in the ring. You can place an urn behind instead, on a tall plinth, to be viewed through the peephole.

Right: Baskets of ivy dress the Post Feature which is self-supporting on its own wide base. Here, it adds grace to a small garden. It also makes an attractive support for a house name or number on the cross-rail.

Left: Mystical, in a ground setting, the Pyramid Lantern highlights interesting plants in the late evening. It can be repositioned when necessary to fit in with the foliage, or it can be raised on a plinth as the plants grow.

Below: Overflowing with plants, the Supertrug still shows its characteristic lines. The handles make it quite easy to be moved about by two people, especially if the plants are in pots, to change your garden display.

Left: Welcome to the lawn, through the Trellis Arch. It is bolted to a pair of stub posts in the grass and to a pair in the flower-bed on the right. Stepping stones preserve the informality.

Below: Clear yacht varnish has been used to show off the natural pine boards of the Pegged Tenon Planter, sited here in a rocky alcove.

Right and below: Nestling in a group of conifers, the Gazebo shows off the diagonal trellis to advantage. The draught screens are folded back to allow side glimpses from the integral seat. The open slatted top allows plenty of sunshine to enter when climbing plants have started to grow. You can have a solid roof if you wish.

A glass of wine and quiet read under a thirty-year-old cherry tree. In this small garden the fence would not allow space for a conventional tree seat. Our Tree Seat solves the problem.

Where the lock and handle need a strong support, tenon an additional vertical board into the rails, as in the lower sketch in Fig. 1. It effectively doubles the thickness of the edge board, when you fix them together with screws.

The frame is best set in concrete. If you make if from large-section timber, it could form end fence posts – at least 100 mm (4 in) square is suggested. Make the top from the same section, so that it matches. Form halving joints to post and at top rails and centre. Cover the joints with a couple of 20 × 150-mm (¾ × 6-in) boards to resist the weather. Saw the top of the gate to blend with the arch and the adjoining sweep of the fence top.

MATERIALS

18 × 69-mm (¾ × 2¾-in) lengths to suit (for all gate construction)

70 × 70 mm (2¾ × 2¾ in) or larger, for posts and top

18 × 44 mm (¾ × 1¾ in), for stop

18 × 145 mm (¾ × 5¾ in), for capping

TOOLS

Cross-cut saw
Jigsaw
Chisels
Plane
Router
Drill
Screwdriver

SMALL GATE

The same idea is continued with this low gate, where the top sweeps down from hinge edge to latch in a gentle line (Fig. 1). The same rules apply, but being smaller, the gate does not need to have the edge boards reinforced. Bear in mind that clearance has to be provided so that the rails or latch board miss the post as the gate swings. This is because the stop strip on the latch post is not in line with the hinge pins.

If you decide to make the small gate very much wider than shown, remember that the diagonal brace will be at a flatter angle. It has to reach at least to the second board in from the edge, and the shaped ends of the brace will need to be much more thinly tapered to sit properly on the horizontal rails. Eventually the brace will not be efficient.

Fig 1

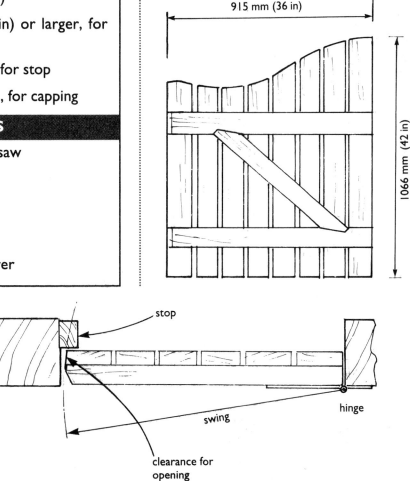

TRELLIS GATE

If you need an openwork gate for a lighter appearance, try this diagonal pattern, based on a Victorian chairback. The main diagonal members provide bracing, and their spacing allows you to make versions of slightly different proportions.

Details are for the gate illustrated only.

You can make it taller or narrower by reducing the gap between the parallel diagonals, or widen it by increasing the gap. Fig. 1 shows the elevation and joint details.

This one has top and bottom rails like a door. Make all the trellis and an inner frame with halving joints, then drop it in and screw it to the uprights and top and bottom rails. Use butt hinges, because strap types will not blend in or fit the pattern. Notice that the tenons are somewhat inset from the top and bottom, to preserve strength.

When you cut mortises in the stiles, leave the wood overlength to avoid breaking out the ends, then trim it to length.

Fig. 1

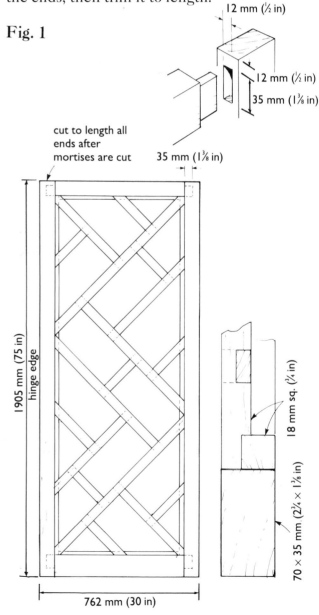

12 mm (½ in)

12 mm (½ in)

35 mm (1⅜ in)

cut to length all ends after mortises are cut

35 mm (1⅜ in)

1905 mm (75 in)

hinge edge

762 mm (30 in)

18 mm sq. (¾ in)

70 × 35 mm (2¾ × 1⅜ in)

MATERIALS

35 × 70 mm (1⅜ × 2¾ in), for the gate uprights (stiles), and top and bottom rails – typically 2 @ 1905 mm (75 in) and 2 @ 726 mm (30 in)

18 × 18 mm (¾ × ¾ in) or 18 × 32 mm (¾ × 1¼ in) for the trellis and its edge strips – about 10 metres (32 ft), depending on spacing

TOOLS

The same kit as for the Tall Gate

FIVE-BAR GATE

CUTTING LIST

Section		No.	Length	
mm	in		mm	in
18 × 71	¾ × 2¾	4	2160	85
		1	2540	100
		2	1066	42
44 × 71	1¾ × 2¾	1	2160	85
50 × 227	2 × 9 sawn	1	1473	58

TOOLS

Cross-cut, tenon and coping saws
Chisels, Drill
Screwdriver, Spanners

You need strong gate posts for this one; it is wide and produces a side load at the hinges. See Fig. 1.

1 Mark out the shape of the hinge stile (the curvy one) on the heavy chunk of timber. When sawn to shape there will be enough waste to make the latch stile.

2 Mark out all the tenons on the 18 × 71 mm (¾ × 2¾ in). They are bare-faced to keep them strong and to avoid mortise clash. Cut them all the same for the bars.

3 Use tenons to set out the mortises in the stiles and on the top rail, which has to go deeper. Form the mortises with chisels or router.

4 Cut rebates (not mortises) for the braces. Note the shapes of the lower end of each. Drill and bolt where shown. The central vertical spacer is only partly set in a rebate in the top rail. Screw it to the three horizontals, then trim it to length – projecting at the bottom where you bolt it. Use stout strap-type hinges with cast sockets on the post.

Fig. 1

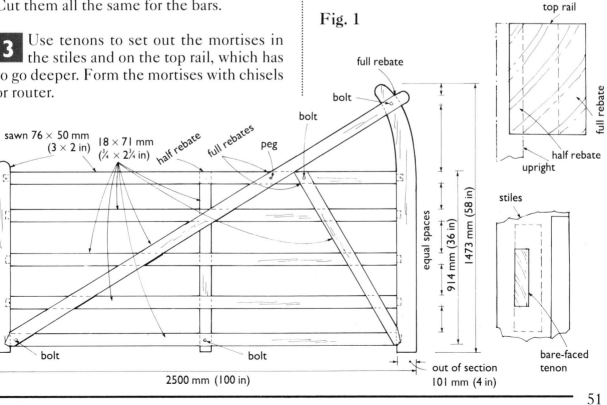

POST LANTERN

If this lamp were to be based exactly on the traditional street lamp it would look too much like a model, so fit decorative plywood brackets to the post top. Both the Post and the lower Pyramid Lanterns are intended to use electric power from a suitably wired indoor source. If you are unsure, get a friendly electrican to advise you and check what you have done.

I am dealing here with the wooden construction and suggest the use of a standard batten-type lamp-holder and weather-resistant cable, attached to an indoor switched plug. The bulb can be either a 40- or a 60-watt type, protected from the weather by sytrene glazing.

CUTTING LIST

Section		No.	Length	
mm	in		mm	in
44 × 69	1¾ × 2¾	1	1232	48½
18 × 69	¾ × 2¾	1	1232	48½
18 × 145	¾ × 5¾	2	254 for cutting	10
18 × 44	¾ × 1¾	4	254	10
35 × 35	1¼ × 1¼	1	203	8
18 × 18	¾ × ¾	1	940 for cutting	37
6	¼ ext. ply	2	610 × 254	24 × 10

TOOLS

Cross-cut saw
Tenon saw
Jigsaw
Router
Chisels
Plane
Drill
Screwdrivers
Wire cutters
Stanley knife

1 Fig. 1 shows the main dimensions and sections. Start by routing a groove for the cable in a strip of 44 × 69 mm (1¾ × 2¾ in). Check that a piece of cable will fit in the groove. It has to be long enough to pass

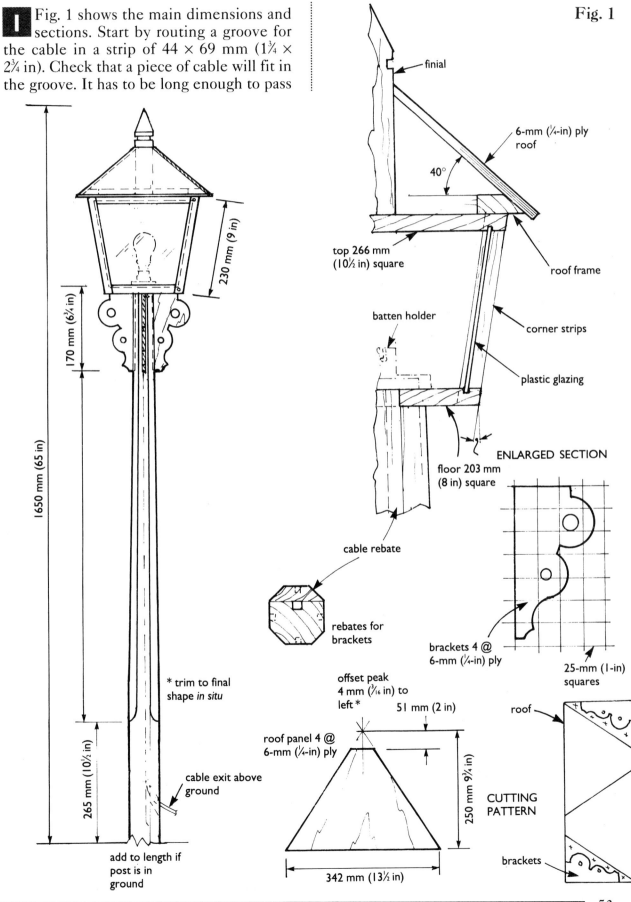

Fig. 1

finial

6-mm (¼-in) ply roof

40°

roof frame

top 266 mm (10½ in) square

batten holder

corner strips

plastic glazing

floor 203 mm (8 in) square

ENLARGED SECTION

cable rebate

rebates for brackets

brackets 4 @ 6-mm (¼-in) ply

25-mm (1-in) squares

230 mm (9 in)

170 mm (6¾ in)

1650 mm (65 in)

* trim to final shape *in situ*

cable exit above ground

265 mm (10½ in)

add to length if post is in ground

offset peak 4 mm (³⁄₁₆ in) to left *

51 mm (2 in)

250 mm 9¾ in

roof panel 4 @ 6-mm (¼-in) ply

342 mm (13½ in)

roof

CUTTING PATTERN

brackets

up to the lamp-holder from the socket in your garage or house, after passing out of sight in an area where it is safe from the lawn mower, spades and feet. Check that the cable can be removed and replaced when a strip of 18 × 69 mm (¾ × 2¾ in) is clamped over the full length of the groove. Remove the cable and glue and pin, or screw this strip in place. Avoid getting globs of glue in the groove.

2 Mark the areas of chamfer and, using the router with a 'V' cutter, make several passes to take of the corners and get an octagonal section (Fig. 2). You can plane these instead and finish the ends with a chisel.

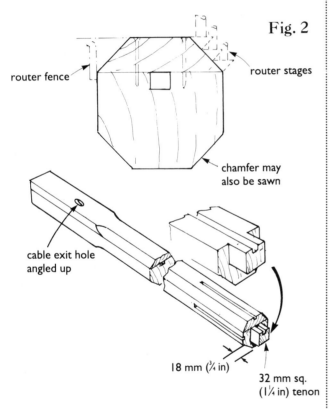

Fig. 2

router fence

router stages

chamfer may also be sawn

cable exit hole angled up

18 mm (¾ in)

32 mm sq. (1¼ in) tenon

3 Rebate for the ply brackets with the router or chisel. Do not go deep in the cover strip, so as to avoid getting through and blocking the cable space. Form a square tenon on the top to fit into the lantern floor.

4 Make the floor from 18-mm-thick (¾-in) board. Glue up to make the width, chamfer to 10 degrees all round and mortise the centre to fit the post tenon.

Check that the cable will go through and down the post when the floor is held in place temporarily.

5 Make the top in a similar form, but larger. Remember that the edges are chamfered down. Saw 18 × 18-mm (¾ × ¾-in) rebates to 10 degrees at each corner of both floor and top.

6 Saw grooves 3 mm (⅛ in) wide and deep down two adjacent sides of the 18 × 18-mm (¾ × ¾-in) strip to take the styrene glazing. Cut the four corner frame strips from this. Position them, grooves inward, in the rebates and mark where the glazing grooves touch. Cut these in the floor and under the top panel (Fig. 3).

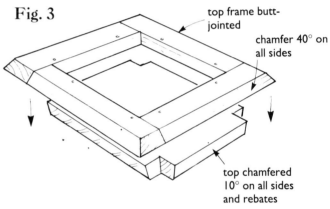

Fig. 3

top frame butt-jointed

chamfer 40° on all sides

top chamfered 10° on all sides and rebates

7 Take the four 18 × 44-mm (¾ × 1¾-in) strips and arrange them to side butt each other at each corner of the top panel (Fig. 4). Glue and pin the top surface, then chamfer the top edges to 40 degrees for the roof panels to sit on.

Fig. 4

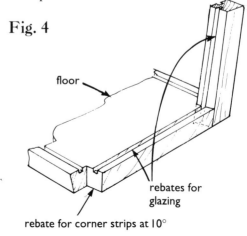

floor

rebates for glazing

rebate for corner strips at 10°

8 Drill through the cover strip on the post 303 mm (12 in) from the bottom, to clear the cable. Angle it upwards with a chisel. Thread the cable through, leaving a little slack, and glue the floor to the post. Fret out the brackets and glue and pin them on. Wire the batten-holder on and screw it to the top. Paint the inside faces of the lantern.

9 Cut the four panels of glazing plastic and use them to align the top over the floor, then glue and screw three corner pieces in place. Just screw the fourth to top and floor. It has to be removable, so that one panel of glazing can be slid out for changing the lamp. Secure the cable to the post at its exit with a cable clamp screwed in place.

10 Cut four roof panels to the shape shown in Fig. 1. Glue and pin these to the top and at each edge. Cut a finial from 34 × 34 mm (1¼ × 1¼ in). Insert it in the centre and glue it to the top panel and roof edges.

Sand the edges of the roof panels and cut narrow strips of 'Flashband' plastic bitumen flashing strip. Apply them to cover each roof corner and around the finial joint (Fig. 5).

The post can be fitted to a short peg driven into the ground, or set in a socket in concrete. Pre-plan for this when selecting the length of the post. Make sure the cable is clear of cutting tools when working. Seal the exit hole with a lump of wax. Painting is up to you, but this project looks good in dark green when set against light evergreen shrubs.

Fig. 5

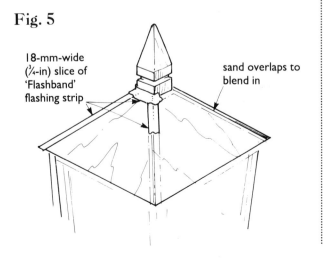

18-mm-wide (¾-in) slice of 'Flashband' flashing strip

sand overlaps to blend in

PYRAMID LANTERN

This project looks impressive in a raised bed among loose foliage. When the plants grow taller the Pyramid Lantern can be raised on a plinth (see page 58). It can be given stability by mounting it on a short wooden spike. It carries a standard bulkhead light unit on a cross-rail to shine upwards.

CUTTING LIST				
Section		No.	Length	
mm	in		mm	in
18 × 145	¾ × 5¾	3	406 for cutting	16
		4	203	8
34 × 34	1¼ × 1¼	4	280	11
18 × 69	¾ × 2¾	1	177	7
18 × 18	¾ × ¾	2	70	2¾

TOOLS
Cross-cut and tenon saws
Chisels
Screwdriver

Fig. 1

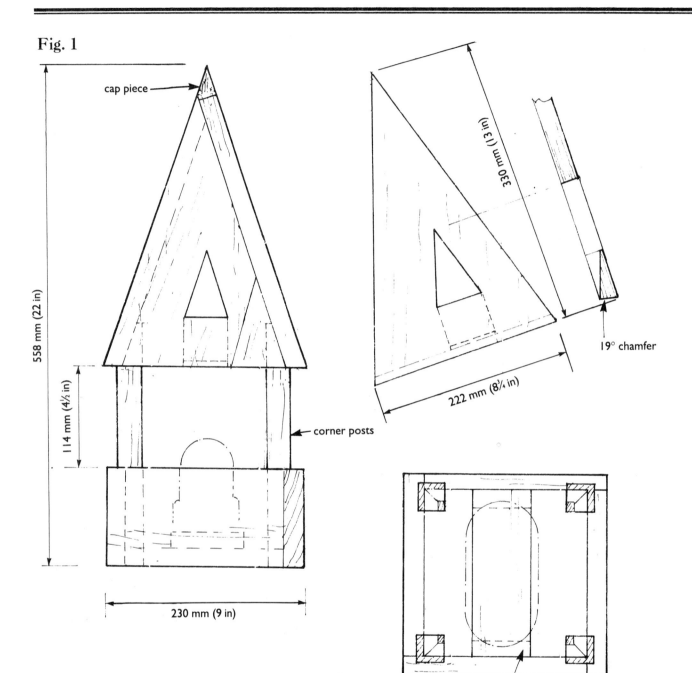

cap piece

558 mm (22 in)

114 mm (4½ in)

corner posts

230 mm (9 in)

330 mm (13 in)

222 mm (8¾ in)

19° chamfer

lamp support batten

TOP VIEW LESS TOP

Fig. 1 shows the elevation and section. The exact size will depend on the size of the lamp unit you choose.

The prototype is made with an inside clearance of 180 mm (7 in) and the base is 18 × 145 mm (¾ × 5¾ in). The same board is used for the top, joined to make up the width and sawn to a triangular shape. All four pieces are the same shape and size, overlapping on one edge for ease of construction. It is also a good test for true 90-degree cutting of the base pieces, because any deviation transferred from piece to piece will multiply the error.

Measure the lamp and decide if the dimensions in Fig. 1 will allow straight transfer to the wood. If so, mark out the wide board, allowing one thickness overlap at one end of each piece. Cut these and transfer the length to one piece of 18 × 145 mm (¾ × 5¾ in), plus a narrow offcut to make up the width. Mark the angle from Fig. 1, which is the true developed shape which suits the angle of the pyramid. You may find it convenient to fit two panels on one wider board made up from three 18 × 145-mm (¾ × 5¾-in) pieces (see Fig. 2).

Fig. 2

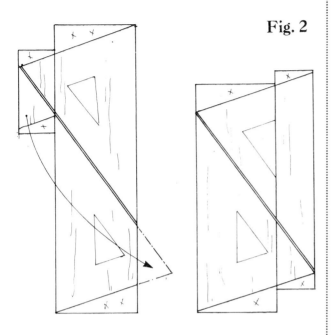

Whichever way you do it, slide the shapes around to avoid as much waste as possible. Having done the marking while the sections of board are temporarily held together with masking tape, glue and cramp them up to set before doing any cutting. (It is much more difficult to cramp up work.)

2 Cut a triangular hole in each panel. It will be off-centre to the wood, but has to be central when assembled. This means

Fig. 3

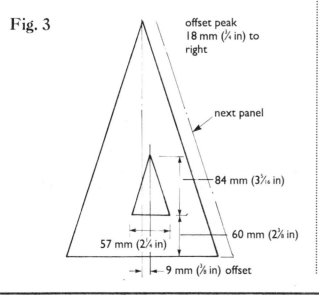

offset peak
18 mm (¾ in) to right

next panel

84 mm (3⁵⁄₁₆ in)

60 mm (2⅜ in)

57 mm (2¼ in)

9 mm (⅜ in) offset

that it should be 9 mm (⅜ in) to the right of the centre when the board overlaps the left one (Fig. 3).

Mark the inside face for identification and carve away the inside lower edge of the hole to allow more light to pass through (Fig. 4).

Fig. 4

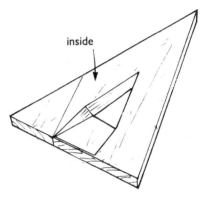

inside

Assembly of the four panels will not be possible without trimming the inside face of the apex so that each overlaps the previous panel without causing the base edge to rock.

3 Glue and pin the four base pieces together, then the four pyramid pieces, carved-side inwards, and overlap to left. When set, plane or sand the corners so that the edge of each overlap is flush. Then sand the uneven top level and cut a scrap piece of 34 × 34 mm (1¼ × 1¼ in) to a double taper to fit in the top hollow. Glue this in and sand it to blend in (Fig. 5).

Fig. 5

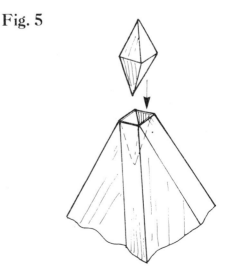

4 Cut the 34 × 34-mm (1¼ × 1¼-in) uprights to length and form a 6-mm (¼-in) rebate on two sides at each end (Fig. 6). These will fit inside the corners of the base. Cut back the top outer edges to a taper from the top rebates.

Fig. 6

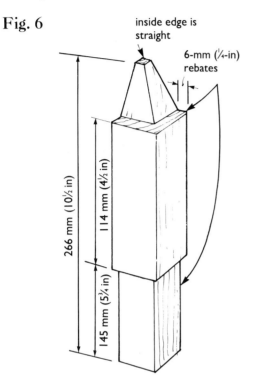

inside edge is straight

6-mm (¼-in) rebates

266 mm (10½ in)

114 mm (4½ in)

145 mm (5¾ in)

This needs doing carefully, so that the angles match the inside tapered corners of the pyramid, and the rebate supports the pyramid when the uprights are glued and pinned into the base corners from the inside. The top will lift off to give access to the lamp.

5 Cut a piece of 18 × 69 mm (¾ × 2¾ in) to fit across inside the base. Screw this to short support pieces of 18 × 18 mm (¾ × ¾ in), glued and pinned inside the sides near the bottom edge. Wire and mount the lamp unit to the 18 × 69 mm and screw this to the supports. Leave the bottom open for drainage.

Paint the lantern white inside and either stain or varnish it outside or paint it white too. Natural wood looks best, but white inside enhances the lighting effect.

PLINTHS

You can make these supports at different heights to raise the pyramid lantern (page 55) as the plants grow round it, or the plinths can be used to support flower urns.

Both types of plinth use the same base and top, as in Fig. 1. The post and brackets

CUTTING LIST				
Section		No.	Length	
mm	in		mm	in
18 × 44	¾ × 1¾	8	254 (short plinth)	10
			406 (tall plinth)	16
32 × 32	1¼ × 1¼	1	342 (short plinth)	13½
			584 (tall plinth)	23½
18 × 71	¾ × 2¾	2	394	15½
		2	71	2¾
18 × 145	¾ × 5¾	2	292	11½

TOOLS
Cross-cut and tenon saws
Chisels
Drill

Fig. 1

are sized to suit. You can make the post go through the base to form a stability spike.

1 Make up identical brackets with angled halving joints and form the ends into tenons. When set, form the tiny tenons at the centre and fit them to 'V' mortises in the post, which has tenons at each end. The longer brackets and post are shown in Fig. 2.

2 Make up the base by overlapping, gluing and screwing the strips, then mark the mortises at dry assembly stage.

Glue and cramp the top together and mark the mortises, which you now cut top and bottom. Just glue and squeeze it together.

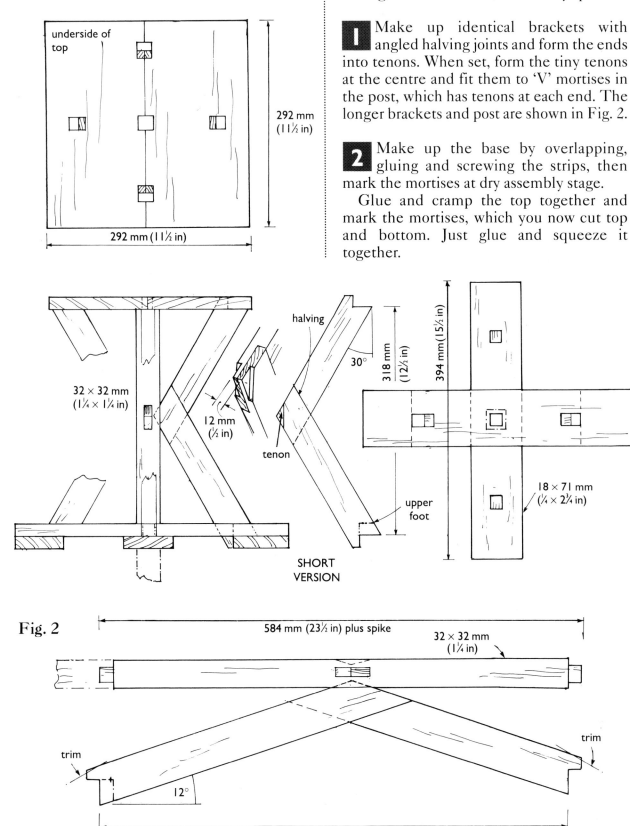

Fig. 2

SUPERTRUG

THIS PLANT BOX teams with a decorative arch and hanging basket. If not too heavily laden with soil – for example, containing potted plants in woodchip – it may be moved about, hence the handles at each end. The sides are shaped in the style of a gardener's trug, though they are much more easily made when it comes to scaling up to the size of this one.

Angled halving joints form the arch in 44 × 44-mm (1¾ × 1¾-in) timber and the ends of the box are strengthened with 18 × 44 mm (¾ × 1¾ in), which forms half the handles. There are also cross-pieces dovetailed in to prevent it spreading. Each of the four dovetails are single types, simple to make, especially if you mark the doublers and sides of the trug from the shape of the batten.

1 Scale up the end shape, shown gridded in Fig. 1, on to the wide board. Cut a pair of sides using a jigsaw, then form a rebate for the ply bottom on the inner face.

You can use either a rebate plane or a router for this job. Now mark the position of the 18 × 44-mm (¾ × 1¾-in) reinforcing pieces, which you can now cut to shape and glue and screw in place from the inside.

2 Shave the handle parts to match the sides and round off the corners of the extreme ends.

Carve the outer edge of the sides at the bottom, slightly rounding as they curve upwards, then blend more roundly at the tips of the handles. Do not go too near the dovetail area.

Fig. 1

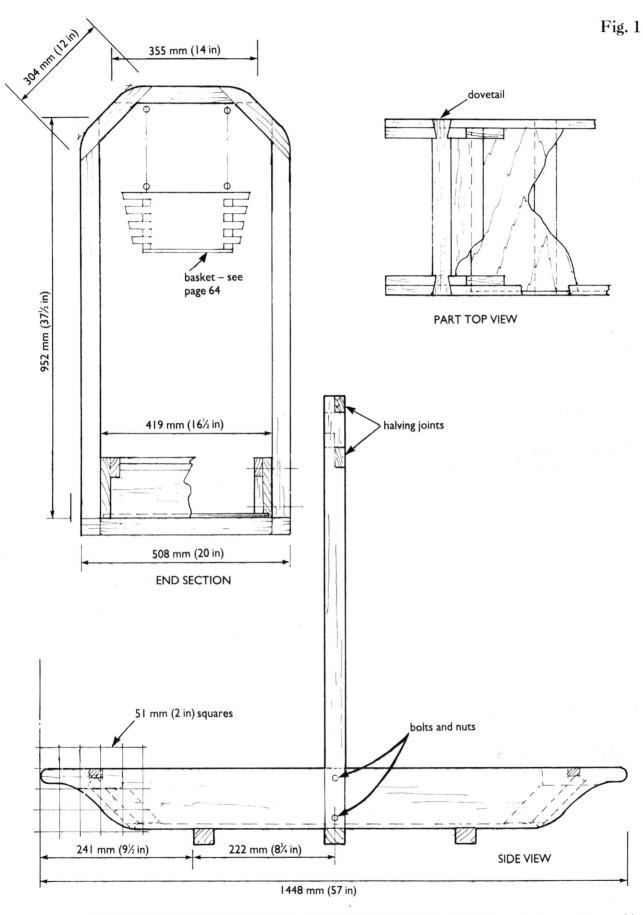

304 mm (12 in)

355 mm (14 in)

dovetail

basket – see
page 64

952 mm (37½ in)

419 mm (16½ in)

PART TOP VIEW

halving joints

508 mm (20 in)

END SECTION

51 mm (2 in) squares

bolts and nuts

241 mm (9½ in)

222 mm (8¾ in)

SIDE VIEW

1448 mm (57 in)

Fig. 2

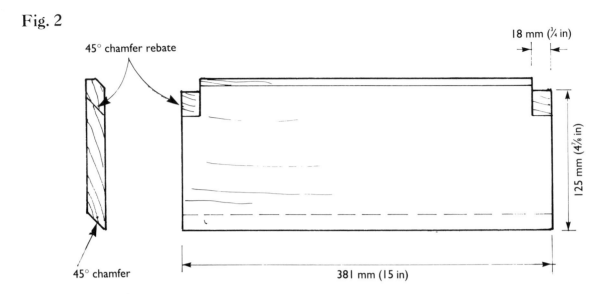

45° chamfer rebate

18 mm (¾ in)

125 mm (4⅞ in)

45° chamfer

381 mm (15 in)

3 Cut a pair of end panels from more wide board and rebate the top corners with a tenon saw and chisel, so that they fit around the horizontal reinforcement when the assembly is on a level surface. The top corner should be 18 mm (¾ in) from the top

of the sides, due to the tilt. Chamfer the bottom edge level with the rebate in each side, then glue and screw them on to the angled reinforcement, as in Fig. 2.

4 Cut two strips of 18 × 44 mm (¾ × 1¾ in) to reach across the outside face of the sides. Saw a dovetail 'pin' at each end to match the thickness of the side and reinforcement pieces. Position the strips over each end board, then mark the 'tails' in the top edge of the side and reinforcement pieces (Fig. 3). Saw on the inside of these lines down to a line scribed to the depth of the strips. Carefully remove the waste with a chisel and try the cross-strip for fit. Adjust with fine chisel strokes for a tight fit and mark to identify each end side and top before gluing in place.

CUTTING LIST				
Section		**No.**	**Length**	
mm	in		mm	in
18 × 145	¾ × 5¾	2	1448	57
		2	381	15
44 × 44	1¾ × 1¾	2	952	37½
		3	355	14
		3	508	20
18 × 44	¾ × 1¾	2	419	16½
		8	203 for cutting	8
9	⅜ ext. ply	1	406 × 1042	16 × 41
TOOLS				
Tenon saw				
Jigsaw or coping saw				
Chisels				
Drill				
Screwdriver				
Rebate plane or router				

Fig. 3

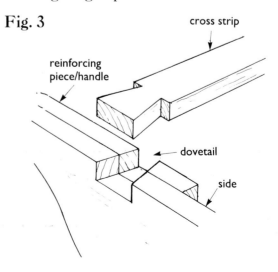

cross strip

reinforcing piece/handle

dovetail

side

5 Cut the bottom from exterior-grade plywood to fit into the rebates in the sides and to cover the chamfer on each angled end board. Glue and screw it in place with roundhead screws. (These do not weaken the edge, as countersunk screws would.) Avoid placing screws at the positions of the outside 44 × 44-mm (1¾ × 1¾-in) cross-battens, which will be added next (see Fig. 4).

Fig. 4

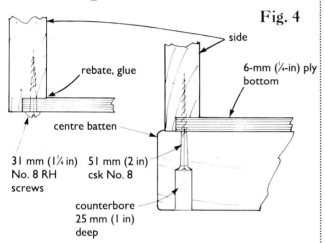

side

rebate, glue

6-mm (¼-in) ply bottom

centre batten

31 mm (1¼ in) No. 8 RH screws

51 mm (2 in) csk No. 8

counterbore 25 mm (1 in) deep

6 Cut two cross-battens to the overall width and a third, 88 mm (3½ in) longer, for the centre position. Counterbore screw holes in these to enable them to be screwed into the sides and to clamp and support the bottom (Fig. 4). Glue them in place as well, to prevent water getting between them and the plywood. Now drill eight drainage holes, 6 mm (¼ in) in diameter, in the bottom, making sure you miss the battens.

7 Make the arch from 44 × 44-mm (1¾ × 1¾-in) wood. Lay it out to match the outside box width and mark out 45-degree halving joints in the top ends of the uprights, the corner pieces and the top pieces (four joints in all). Form the joints with a tenon saw and chisel, or use a router. Glue and screw these. Round off the corners a little to form a pleasing shape, but do not take too much off the joints.

8 Drive a No. 10 50-mm (2-in) screw into each top edge of the projecting centre batten and cut off the head to form a peg. Position the arch over these and give it a tap

Fig. 5

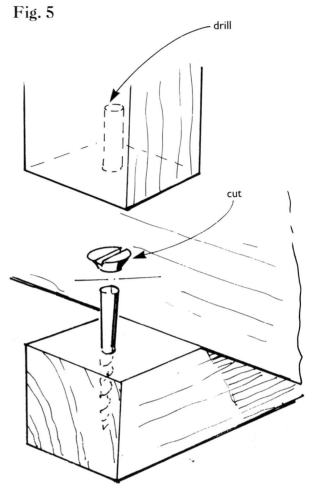

drill

cut

to mark for drilling, as in Fig. 5. Drill to fit to provide location. Now, with the arch checked for the vertical, drill through the uprights and box sides as shown in Fig. 1, so that 6 × 70-mm (¼ × 2¾-in) bolts and nuts can be used to secure it.

Put the nuts (heavily greased or waxed) on the inside of the box, and ensure that the bolts can be slid out, yet are not so free in the holes as to permit wobble. The arch can then be removed for storage or to make it easier to plant out the box.

9 Treat the inside thoroughly with preservative and the outside with either preservative stain, varnish or microporous paint. Fit hooks for a hanging basket or box, which is the next part of this project.

It can also be used with some of the other items, such as arches, pergolas and post features.

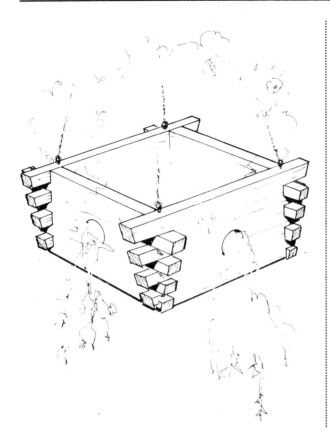

HANGING BASKET

This small item can be either something to use up bits of wood, if done as a one-off, or the start of a trend, if you get into the rhythm of it. Fig. 1 shows its simplicity, yet the finger-jointed corners make it decorative at times when the plants have yet to cascade over the edges. The corners will still peep through the foliage as the season progresses. There is a hole in the centre of each side so that trailing plants can be popped in. The sides are straight for simplicity, and the corners slope.

1 Make a template from hardboard or scrap ply, as in Fig. 2. This carries the end angles and the positions of hole centres. The holes will help to form the joint fingers.

2 Mark out the sides on 18×145-mm ($\frac{3}{4} \times 5\frac{3}{4}$-in) board as shown in Fig. 3. Use a flat bit to stop each slot, cut the board into sections, then saw in to meet the holes with

Fig. 1

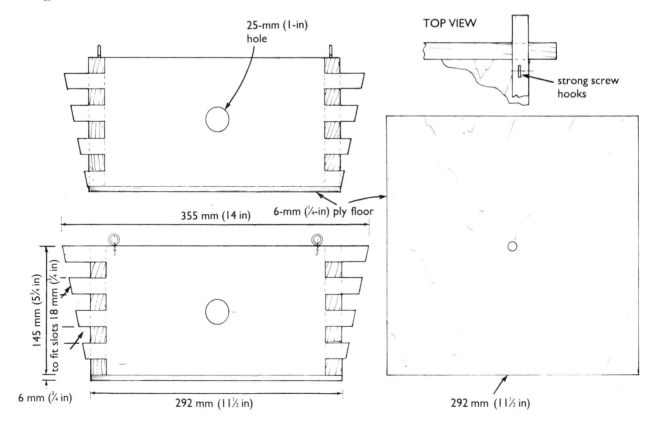

25-mm (1-in) hole

TOP VIEW

strong screw hooks

355 mm (14 in)

6-mm (¼-in) ply floor

145 mm (5¼ in)

18 mm (¾ in)

to fit slots

6 mm (¾ in)

292 mm (11½ in)

292 mm (11½ in)

Fig. 2

a tenon saw or jigsaw. Finally square up the inside corners with a chisel. Saw the remaining rebate at top or bottom, as marked. You will find that two sides have

this rebate on the long top edge and the other two have them on the bottom edge. When the box is assembled the fingers interlock.

3 Check that all the corner fingers sit snugly in the adjacent side recesses. Mark them for reference, then clean up and glue them to form the box.

4 Cut the bottom to the outside face dimensions and glue and nail it in place. Run a fillet of glue down all the inside corners and around the bottom joint. Drill a

Fig. 3

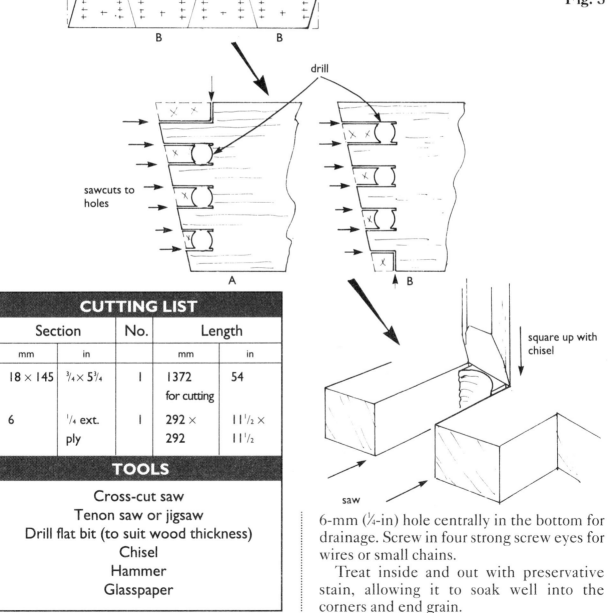

CUTTING LIST				
Section		No.	Length	
mm	in		mm	in
18 × 145	¾ × 5¾	1	1372 for cutting	54
6	¼ ext. ply	1	292 × 292	11½ × 11½

TOOLS
Cross-cut saw
Tenon saw or jigsaw
Drill flat bit (to suit wood thickness)
Chisel
Hammer
Glasspaper

6-mm (¼-in) hole centrally in the bottom for drainage. Screw in four strong screw eyes for wires or small chains.

Treat inside and out with preservative stain, allowing it to soak well into the corners and end grain.

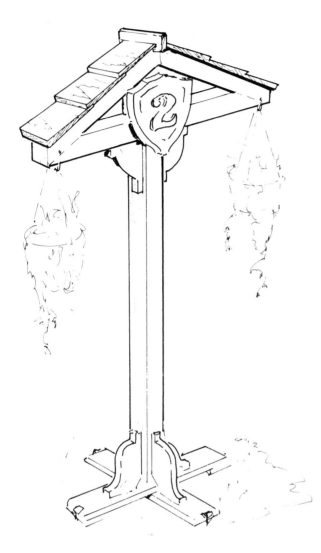

Fig. 1

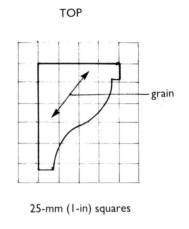

TOP

grain

25-mm (1-in) squares

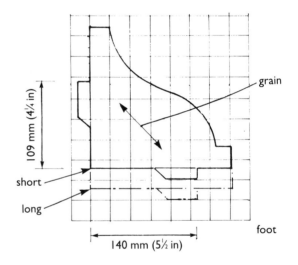

109 mm (4¼ in)

grain

short

long

140 mm (5½ in)

foot

THIS DECORATIVE FEATURE is intended to be used as a house-name/number or hanging-basket support. It has a foot for use on hard surfaces, yet may be sited as a post in a ground socket or pre-driven hole. Where there is already paving, additional stability can be given by metal hooks between the slabs.

Heavy hanging baskets will add considerably to the stability of this project because they impose a powerful down-load on the base to brace it against wind thrust on the upper part.

The baskets swing a little to absorb gusts, but not so much as to unbalance it. If severe gales are forecast, it is a simple matter to lay the post out flat, although the prototype has survived high winds, unscathed, in level grass.

1 Copy the gridded shapes (Fig. 1) for the brackets shown in Fig. 2 on to the wide board and cut them with a jigsaw. Note that the grain direction gives them strength and enables them to be drawn on the width of the board without joints. If your wood is a little undersized, a small piece missing from the inside corner will not affect the strength.

Reduce the width of the tenons in each lower bracket to 9 mm (⅜ in) with a tenon saw and chisel or router.

2 Make the post from 70 × 70 mm (2¾ × 2¾ in) and double chamfer the top to 30 degrees. Form haunched mortises in the lower end of the post on all sides. Reduce the bottom end to form a 25 × 25-mm (1 × 1-in) stub tenon, which will locate in the base (Fig. 3 overleaf).

Fig. 2

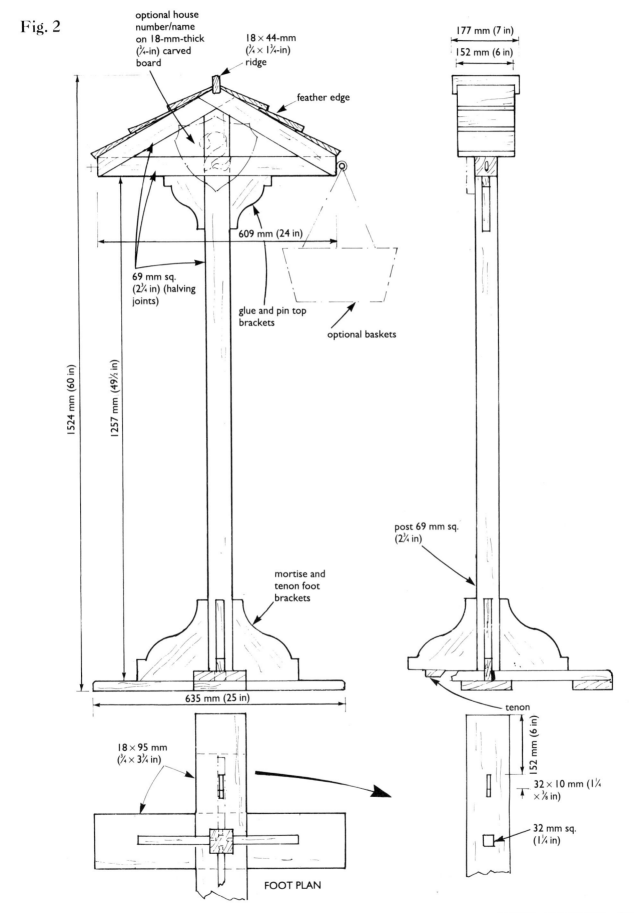

optional house number/name on 18-mm-thick (¾-in) carved board

18 × 44-mm (¾ × 1¾-in) ridge

feather edge

609 mm (24 in)

69 mm sq. (2¾ in) (halving joints)

glue and pin top brackets

optional baskets

1524 mm (60 in)

1257 mm (49½ in)

mortise and tenon foot brackets

177 mm (7 in)

152 mm (6 in)

post 69 mm sq. (2¾ in)

tenon

635 mm (25 in)

18 × 95 mm (¾ × 3¾ in)

FOOT PLAN

152 mm (6 in)

32 × 10 mm (1¼ × ⅜ in)

32 mm sq. (1¼ in)

Fig. 3

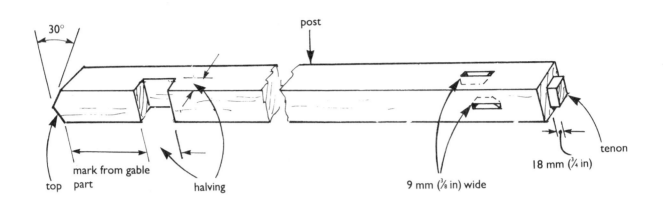

3 Using more 70 × 70 mm (2¾ × 2¾ in), make a 30-degree gable shape with halved joints all round (more sawing or routing). Position it to sit on the chamfered post top and mark out and cut a halving joint to the post at the bottom centre. Glue all these joints.

CUTTING LIST				
Section		No.	Length	
mm	in		m/mm	ft/in
70 × 70	2¾ × 2¾	1	3 metres for cutting	9 ft 9in
18 × 145	¾ × 5¾	1	1423 for cutting	56
Feather edge				
150	6	1	1 metre	3 ft 3 in
18 × 44	¾ × 1¾	1	177	7
TOOLS				

Saw
Tenon saw
Jigsaw or coping saw
Drill
Chisels
Screwdriver
Hammer
Router (optional)

4 To make the base, screw and glue two strips of wide board over each other, then make up the thickness under the ends of the upper one, so that it stands level. Cut a mortise to fit the post end and four more measured from the bottom brackets. The inner ends of these slope to match the tenons on the brackets.

5 Cut short pieces of feather edge board to form shingles, and nail them to the gable. Screw the top of the upper pair in pre-drilled holes to avoid splitting. Add a dummy ridge piece from 18 × 44 mm (¾ × 1¾ in), by sawing a shallow rebate in the top.

6 Glue and pin the top brackets in place and glue the lower set to the post. Insert all five tenons into the base and glue them and the meeting faces of the brackets themselves. You can put additional screws in from underneath either now or later to clamp the job.

7 Design your own panel to carry the house name or number. Carve or rout the name panel in a board of suitable width and screw it in place from the back of the post. It looks best in a natural varnish or varnish-stain finish. The shingles, however, can take a darker shade of preservative stain, or you can sand off their natural sawn surface and varnish them.

GARDEN SHELVES

CUTTING LIST				
Section		No.	Length	
mm	in		mm	in
12 × 44	½ × 1¾	1	1524	60
18 × 44	¾ × 1¾	1	122	48
32 × 95	1¾ × 3¾	6	1193	47
44 × 44	1¾ × 1¾	4	1193	47

TOOLS

Cross-cut and tenon saws
Chisels
Drill
Screwdriver

Easy to make, these shelves, with optional front boards, can be used for storage or display. Fig. 1 shows the entire project.

1 Lay the 44 × 44 mm (1¾ × 1¾ in) down to form the ends at the angles shown. Mark and cut the angles halving at the apex, then trim the back leg so that it is vertical against the wall or fence. Now mark and form all the shallow rebates for the shelf rails and brace. Note that the brace uses one edge as part of a crude dovetail.

2 Cut up the 18 × 44 mm (¾ × 1¾ in) to form shelf bearers of the appropriate length. Glue and screw these to the legs,

allowing space above each for the shelf strips in the same rebate.

3 Screw all the shelf strips to the rails and, if you wish, add facings of whatever width you require to the front edge of the shelves using the 18-mm (¾-in) thick board.

4 Screw strong mirror plates to the back legs near the top so that you can fix it firmly to a wall or fence. It is quite stable as it is, but someone might clout it with the barrow! You can stain the shelves with preservative or paint them.

Fig. 1

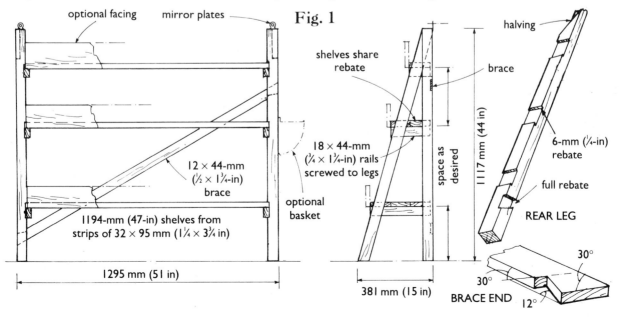

optional facing   mirror plates

shelves share rebate

brace

halving

18 × 44-mm (¾ × 1¾-in) rails screwed to legs

optional basket

6-mm (¼-in) rebate

full rebate

REAR LEG

1117 mm (44 in)

space as desired

12 × 44-mm (½ × 1¾-in) brace

1194-mm (47-in) shelves from strips of 32 × 95 mm (1¼ × 3¾ in)

1295 mm (51 in)

381 mm (15 in)

30°
30°
12°
BRACE END

GARDEN TOOL STORE

THIS STORAGE project should be big enough to house a small mower and hand tools such as a spade, fork, hoe, etc. There will not be much room left for things like sacks of potting compound. Use feather edge board to clad the wall and put felt on the plywood roof, all as in Fig. 1.

1 Make a bottom frame with halved joints 18 × 44 (¾ × 1¾ in). Form rebates at these points to take the rebated posts, which are 32 × 32 mm (1¼ in).

2 Fit the posts dry and make the gable boards from 18 × 195 mm (¾ × 5¾ in). Join the posts with these and with ply gussets cut from the smaller pieces and then trimmed to the roof angle.

You now have a front and a back ready for the bottom. There is no floor – use 12-mm (½-in) ply if you want one, or stand it on paving.

3 Nail feather edge boards all round the sides and back and on the door, after making the 18 × 44-mm (¾ × 1¾-in) outline, halved again, at each corner. The frame is made up flat so that the boards are nailed on to the 44-mm (1¾-in) face.

CUTTING LIST

Section		No.	Length	
mm	in		mm	in
18 × 44	¾ × 1¾	5	915	36
		6	508	20
		2	1600	63
32 × 32	1¼ × 1¼	4	1676	66
18 × 195	¾ × 5¾	2	1066	42
18 × 192	¾ × 5½	24	915 feather edge	36
		24	508	20
6	¼ ext. ply	2	585 × 585	23 × 23
		2	134 × 134	12 × 12

TOOLS

Cross-cut and tenon saws
Chisels
Drill
Screwdriver
Hammer

Fig. 1

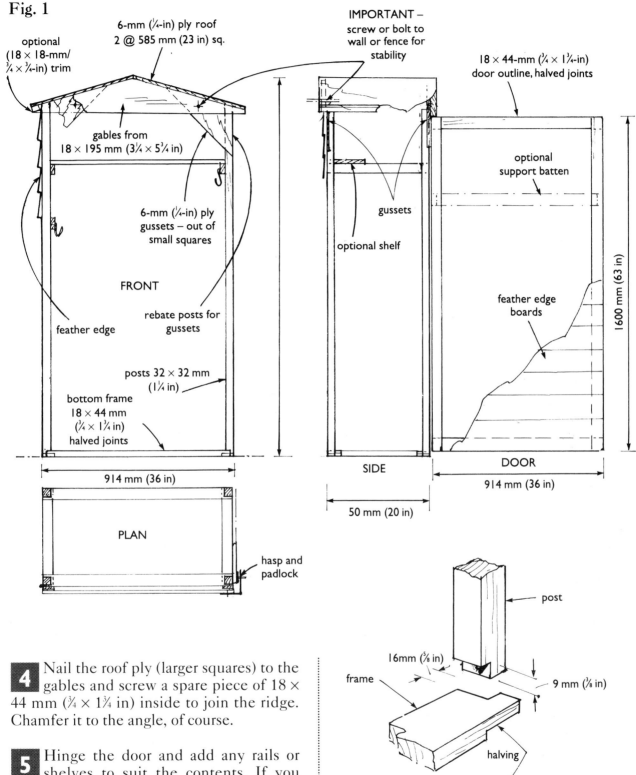

optional
(18 × 18-mm/
¾ × ¾-in) trim

6-mm (¼-in) ply roof
2 @ 585 mm (23 in) sq.

gables from
18 × 195 mm (3¾ × 5¾ in)

6-mm (¼-in) ply
gussets – out of
small squares

FRONT

feather edge

rebate posts for
gussets

posts 32 × 32 mm
(1¼ in)

bottom frame
18 × 44 mm
(¾ × 1¾ in)
halved joints

914 mm (36 in)

PLAN

hasp and
padlock

IMPORTANT –
screw or bolt to
wall or fence for
stability

18 × 44-mm (¾ × 1¾-in)
door outline, halved joints

gussets

optional shelf

SIDE

50 mm (20 in)

optional
support batten

feather edge
boards

DOOR

914 mm (36 in)

1600 mm (63 in)

post

16mm (⅝ in)

frame

9 mm (⅜ in)

halving

frame

4 Nail the roof ply (larger squares) to the gables and screw a spare piece of 18 × 44 mm (¾ × 1¾ in) inside to join the ridge. Chamfer it to the angle, of course.

5 Hinge the door and add any rails or shelves to suit the contents. If you decide to hang heavy tools like spades and forks on the door, position them close to the hinge edge – otherwise the whole thing is likely to tilt. This project will blend in well with the garden when treated with preservative stain.

THREE ARCHES

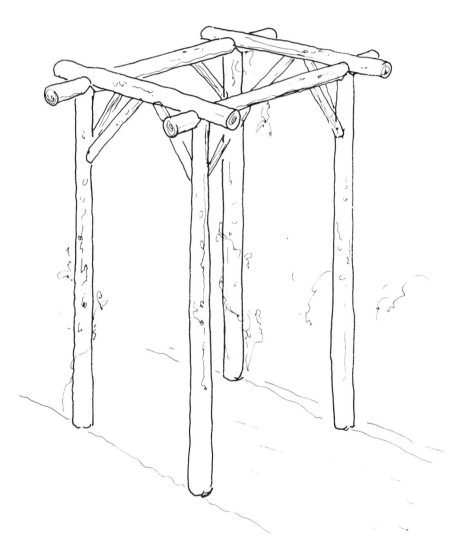

SEVERAL ARCHES are shown here. The most traditional type is made from larch poles, more likely to be found in garden centres than in woodyards. The choice is fairly limited these days; it is no longer so easy to find 'bean poles' and 'laths' for garden work. It seems that the pursuit of the 'instant garden effect' has been more profitable for the trade than the sale of materials.

RUSTIC ARCH

The poles are generally long enough to set in concrete, but they might even be shaped to fit metal post sockets driven in. Fig. 1 shows typical dimensions for a rustic arch with braces. The important feature is the design of the joints, which are shaped so that water does not gather in hollows and air can circulate to dry them (Fig. 2). All hollowed cuts are underneath and the rounded or pointed parts face upwards. Nail the braces into shaped notches, designed to wedge the braces in place once all the nails are in position.

Make the braces first. Shape the top joints, whittling away any bark that will come within the joint. If you cut the joints cleanly, they could be fixed with waterproof glue in addition to nailing. Form the notches for the braces *in situ*, after checking that everything is set up square. The reason for this is that you will probably need to set the posts in their holes before you join everything up.

Fig. 1

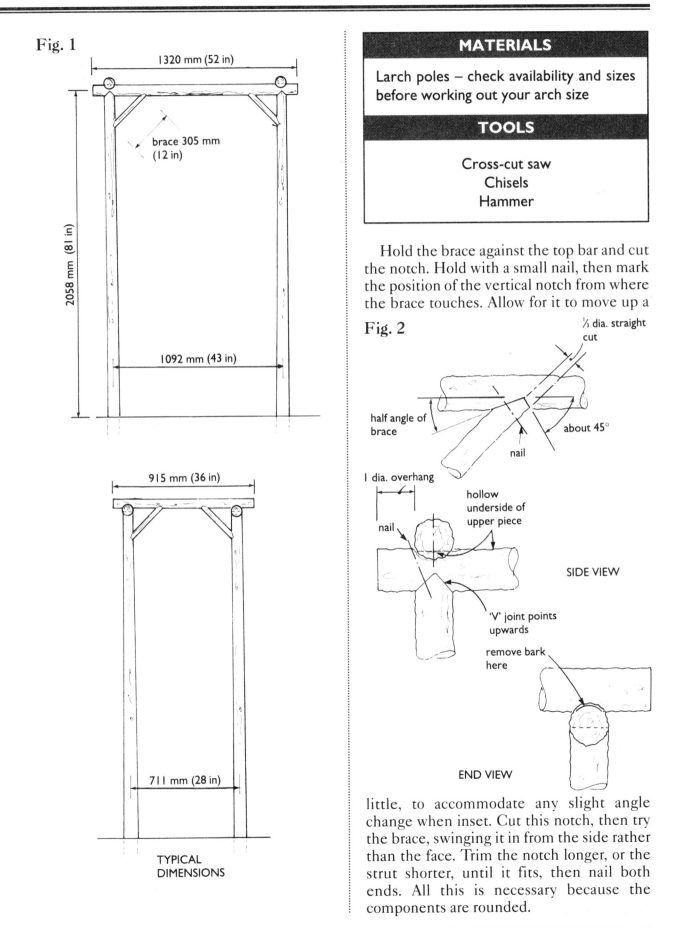

1320 mm (52 in)

brace 305 mm (12 in)

2058 mm (81 in)

1092 mm (43 in)

915 mm (36 in)

711 mm (28 in)

TYPICAL
DIMENSIONS

MATERIALS

Larch poles – check availability and sizes before working out your arch size

TOOLS

Cross-cut saw
Chisels
Hammer

Hold the brace against the top bar and cut the notch. Hold with a small nail, then mark the position of the vertical notch from where the brace touches. Allow for it to move up a

Fig. 2

⅓ dia. straight cut

half angle of brace

about 45°

nail

I dia. overhang

nail

hollow underside of upper piece

SIDE VIEW

'V' joint points upwards

remove bark here

END VIEW

little, to accommodate any slight angle change when inset. Cut this notch, then try the brace, swinging it in from the side rather than the face. Trim the notch longer, or the strut shorter, until it fits, then nail both ends. All this is necessary because the components are rounded.

BRACED ARCH

Make this one from sawn sections or PAR timber. The outriggers carry hanging baskets and braces outside the uprights. This gives headroom within the arch.

This project involves certain joints that need the rough sawn finish of the timber to be smoothed where glue is to be introduced. Fig. 1 gives the dimensions. The joints between the boards which form the top and the posts are shown in Fig. 2. Note also that the braces are tenoned into the posts but rebated to fit the cross-piece.

If you wish, this arch can stand up without being set into the ground. The extra gussets dowelled to the top boards add rigidity. If the arch is in a windy situation, set stakes in the ground and bolt them to the side of the posts. Then, if they rot later, they can be replaced without anyone having to take the arch down. Established climbing plants may also help to fix the arch.

Fig. 1

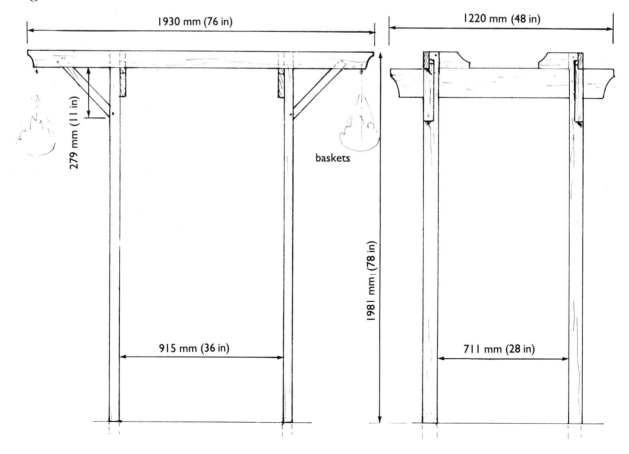

Fig. 2

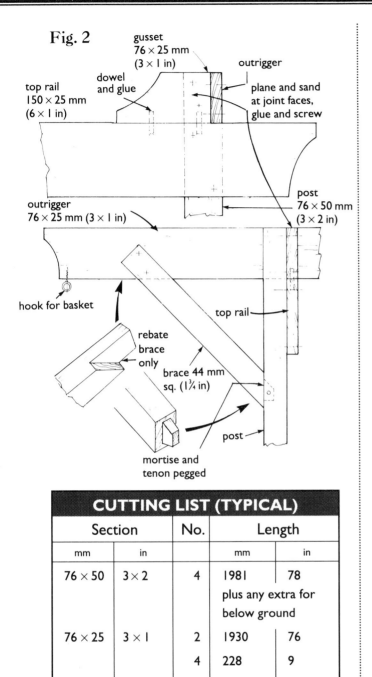

gusset
76 × 25 mm
(3 × 1 in)

outrigger

top rail
150 × 25 mm
(6 × 1 in)

dowel
and glue

plane and sand
at joint faces,
glue and screw

outrigger
76 × 25 mm (3 × 1 in)

post
76 × 50 mm
(3 × 2 in)

hook for basket

top rail

rebate
brace
only

brace 44 mm
sq. (1¼ in)

post

mortise and
tenon pegged

CUTTING LIST (TYPICAL)					
Section		No.	Length		
mm	in		mm	in	
76 × 50	3 × 2	4	1981 plus any extra for below ground	78	
76 × 25	3 × 1	2	1930	76	
		4	228	9	
150 × 25	6 × 1	2	1220	48	
51 × 51	2 × 2	4	330	13	

TOOLS

Cross-cut saw and tenon saw
Jigsaw
Chisels
Plane
Screwdriver
Drill
Hammer

If you prefer to incorporate trellis for a more decorative effect, use a panel of diagonal 18 × 18-mm (¾ × ¾-in) or 18 × 12-mm (¾ × ½-in) strips 500 mm (20 in) deep across the upper sides. This will brace the arch and obviate the need for the gussets referred to earlier (Fig. 3). The upper and lower framing strips for the diagonal trellis not only look better if they are made from a larger section than the trellis, but will afford more space for woodscrews at each post.

Fig. 3

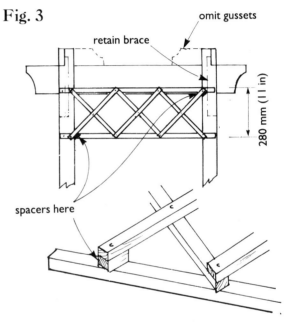

omit gussets

retain brace

280 mm (11 in)

spacers here

WATCHPOINT

If you have to site an arch on sloping ground, remember to mark the posts, which will be of different lengths, so that you assemble them correctly.

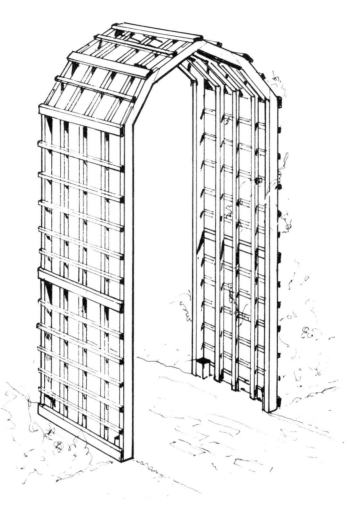

TRELLIS ARCH

Square trellis is easier to fit on this five-jointed arch. All the vertical elements of the trellis combine with 18 × 44-mm (¾ × 1¾-in) front and rear frames, which are connected with halving joints to make a light but rigid unit. Fig. 1 shows the main dimensions and method of pegging it down to renewable stub posts. The latter can go through gravel or grass, but if the path is as wide as the arch, or if the area is paved or concreted, you need to leave holes for them.

TOOLS

Cross-cut and tenon saws
Chisels
Drill
Router (optional)
Screwdriver
Hammer

CUTTING LIST (TYPICAL)

Section		No.	Length	
mm	in		mm	in
18 × 44	¾ × 1¾	4	1892	74½
		9	660	26
		8	483	19
18 × 18	¾ × ¾	6	1829	72
		12	483	19
		24	660	26
			plus pegs and rough battens	

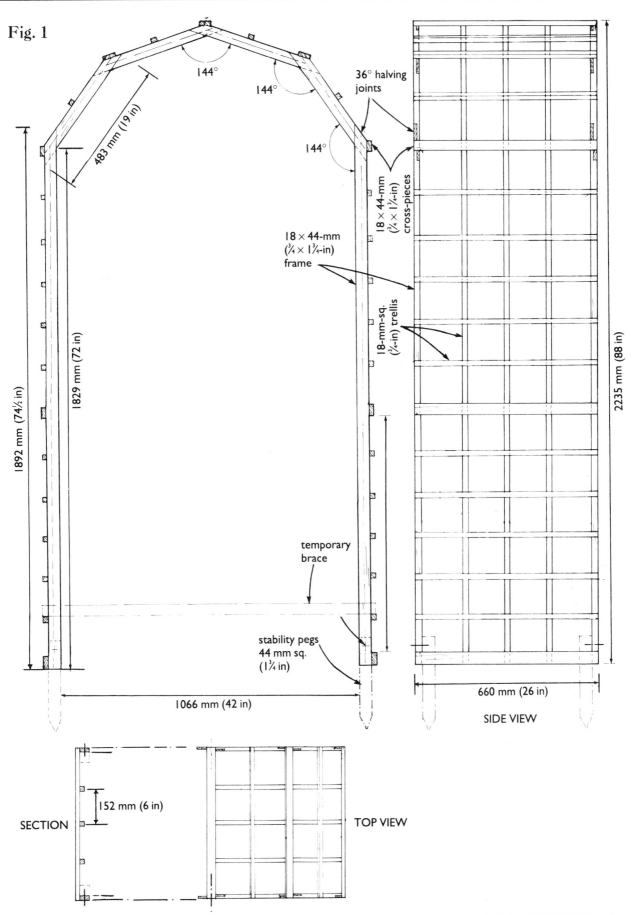

Fig. 1

144°

144°

144°

483 mm (19 in)

36° halving joints

18 × 44-mm (¾ × 1¾-in) cross-pieces

18 × 44-mm (¾ × 1¾-in) frame

18-mm-sq. (¾-in) trellis

1892 mm (74½ in)

1829 mm (72 in)

2235 mm (88 in)

temporary brace

stability pegs 44 mm sq. (1¾ in)

1066 mm (42 in)

660 mm (26 in)

SIDE VIEW

152 mm (6 in)

SECTION

TOP VIEW

1 Form halving joints on all the 18 × 44-mm (¾ × 1¾-in) frames. Fig. 2 shows the angles for cutting the joints. Remember that one of the top pieces has both halvings on one face, whereas the others have one on each alternate face.

Fig. 2

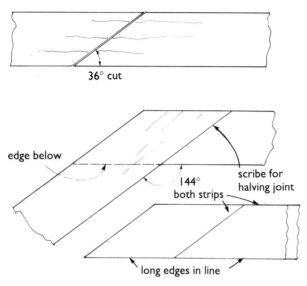

36° cut

edge below

144°
both strips

scribe for halving joint

long edges in line

2 Lay one frame flat and tack a brace across to keep it firm. Rest it on scrap packing to maintain an even distance above the floor (Fig. 3). This is to enable you to turn a screwdriver easily without scraping your knuckles on the floor. Cut all the 18 × 44-mm (¾ × 1¾-in) cross-pieces to length and, using a square, glue and screw them at the junctions on the outside edge. Then fix the other frame to their upper ends (Fig. 4).

Fig. 3

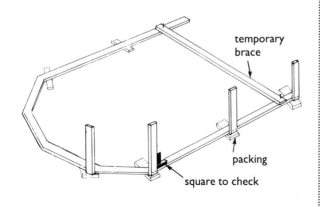

temporary brace

packing

square to check

Fig. 4

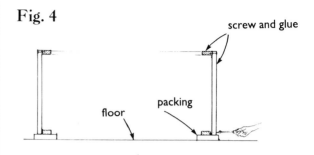

screw and glue

floor

packing

3 Continue by making halving joints in the ends of the 18 × 18-mm (¾ × ¾-in) trellis members that run parallel to the frames. When the glue is set, insert them in the structure and tie them on one side while nailing them to the 18 × 44-mm (¾ × 1¾-in) cross-pieces, as in Fig. 5. Thread the short cross-trellis pieces under them while they rest on the floor, and nail (and, if you wish) glue them to the first set. This completes the side panels.

Fig. 5

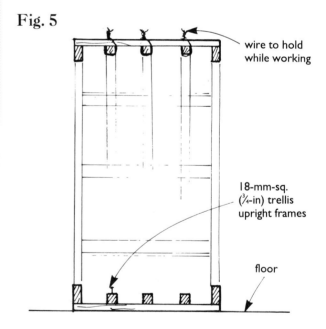

wire to hold while working

18-mm-sq. (¾-in) trellis upright frames

floor

4 Drill and screw through the halving joints of the trellis into the top three cross-pieces, as in Fig. 6. Now rest each top panel on a firm support, such as an angled board, or tilt the arch base up and use the floor. Cut the cross-trellis strips and nail through into them. Turn the arch on its back and nail each cross-trellis strip to the edge of the main frames.

Fig. 6

pre-drill, nail
and glue
through joints   nail and glue

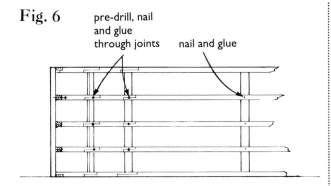

5 Measure the distance between each upright and knock up a rectangular frame, as in Fig. 7. Use this to site and space the supports, which have to be driven almost to ground or path level. Check that they are all level across the tops by placing a spirit level on a batten over them in the order shown in Fig. 8.

Screw or bolt the arch to the supports. Make sure that the frames are upright with the level when positioning the holes. If the ground is level from side to side and from front to back, insert packing to bring the arch just off the ground (to resist rot). If the ground slopes, you will need wedges to do this at the three lower corners. Only when the arch is vertical drill for bolts or screws.

Fig. 7

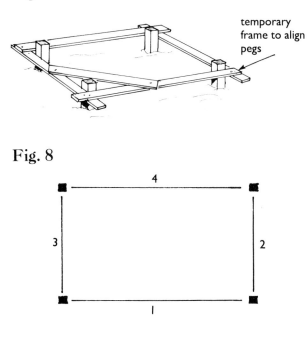

temporary
frame to align
pegs

Fig. 8

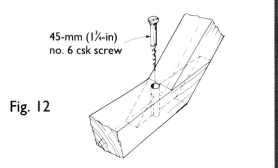

TIPS

When nailing, remember to use a heavy mallet to place behind joints that are otherwise unsupported (Fig. 9).

Fig. 9

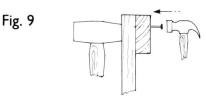

Blunt the nail points by tapping them with the hammer while the nail is head down on a hard surface. This makes the nail cut, rather than split, the wood fibres (Fig. 10).

Fig. 10

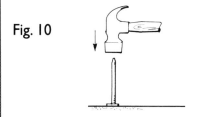

Tack a light supporting batten to each of the half jointed 18 × 18-mm (¾ × ¾-in) trellis assemblies when positioning them for fixing to the main arch. They are quite flexible and the joints might otherwise be strained (Fig. 11).

Fig. 11

Be sure to drill a clearance hole right through the halving joint, as in Fig. 12. A tight fit will force the glue apart.

45-mm (1¼-in)
no. 6 csk screw

Fig. 12

THREE PERGOLAS

TRADITIONAL PERGOLAS are intended to be an architectural addition to the garden or house. If they are heavily covered by foliage, their interesting outline will be lost.

A good pergola will provide attractive patterns of light and shade and give importance to a pathway or patio. This latter application is the simplest, as it gets partial support from the house. Pergolas are best kept plain if the house is contemporary, but the horizontal members may be crossed over or extended slightly and given decorative shaping at the ends. Those in open parts of the garden need some purpose, like acting as a stop to a lawn. Such a pergola may be just a single row of frames. Highlight a pathway with a double row, or make a short, wide type to frame a vista.

Choose a level site, for stepped pergolas are more difficult to detail. It is worth landscaping the area to deal with this. Curved walks give opportunities for changing views as the pergola sweeps round. All the projects described here are structural only, because each individual site will dictate specific length and shape.

LEAN-TO PERGOLA

Build the bare post and cross-frame from sawn timber from 50 × 75 mm (2 × 3 in) to 100 × 100 mm (4 × 4 in). For the posts shown, use 25 × 150 mm (1 × 6 in) for the frame. Screw or bolt it to the posts flush with the top, as in Fig. 1. The height should be about 2.4 metres (just under 8 ft) and the spacing about 1.5 metres (just under 5 ft). It is convenient to arrange the spacing so that fixing lugs can be placed in paving-slab joints. The base of each post is clear of the ground, to avoid rot, so drill and screw in a

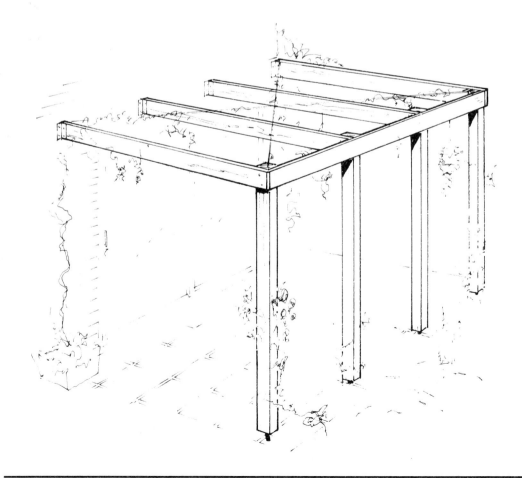

Fig. 1

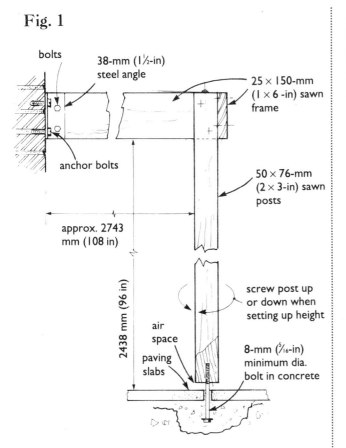

bolts

38-mm (1½-in) steel angle

25 × 150-mm (1 × 6 -in) sawn frame

anchor bolts

50 × 76-mm (2 × 3-in) sawn posts

approx. 2743 mm (108 in)

2438 mm (96 in)

screw post up or down when setting up height

air space

paving slabs

8-mm (⁵⁄₁₆-in) minimum dia. bolt in concrete

TOOLS

The Lean-to Pergola will need only a cross-cut and possibly a jigsaw, and then chisel, drill and screwdriver.

The other two require the same list of tools and timber sizes given for the Braced Arch (see page 80).

Fig. 2

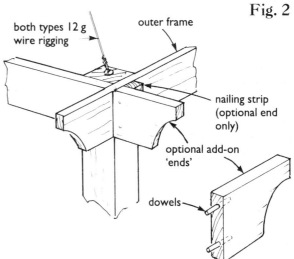

both types 12 g wire rigging

outer frame

nailing strip (optional end only)

optional add-on 'ends'

dowels

bolt or length of thick-screwed rod. Secure it with a nut or the bolt head and large washer in concrete below the slab level. Thus posts can be replaced without disturbing the paving or wall.

Attach the house ends of the top rails to the wall with steel angle strip. Screw or bolt the strip to the timber and use expanding fixing bolts for the wall. Rig steel cross-wires from corner to corner across the top, to make it rigid. You can train creepers along them.

Should you wish to add decorative ends to the frame, follow Fig. 2. Saw the shapes with a jigsaw and dowel them to the structure. Add a vertical strip of 32 × 32 mm (1¼ × 1¼ in) to strengthen the joint. Screw into it from both pieces. Site these on the least seen side of the frames. A deep halving joint may look neater, but in this case it weakens the outer frame member.

As pergolas of this type are often near patio doors, there is not much to get hold of. Be careful when erecting the pergola, if you do not have a helper to steady things.

However, this prototype was done single-handed by using one screw at each point in the wall and front strip, then swinging each piece up into positon in the order shown in Fig. 3. Having done this, and secured straining wires across the corners, the remaining screws were put in and the temporary braces removed.

Fig. 3

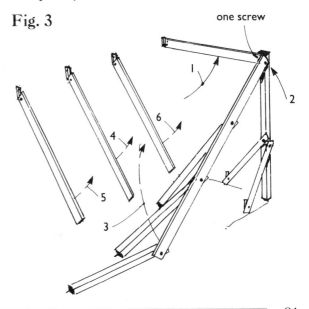

one screw

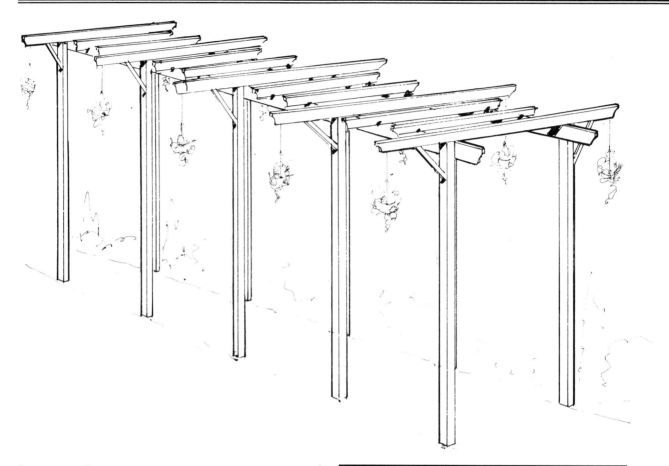

Long Pergola

This pergola is an extended version of the Braced Arch (see page 80). Fig. 1 shows one bay and the joints which support intermediate cross-rails.

This is quite a light-looking structure, with 50 × 75-mm (2 × 3-in) posts and long 25 × 150-mm (1 × 6-in) rails. The outrigger cross-rails are 25 × 100 mm (1 × 4 in) and their braces are as in that arch project.

Screw 25 × 25-mm (1 × 1-in) vertical strips to the inside faces of the long rails to project up 100 mm (4 in). Cut the intermediate cross-pieces shorter, but shape the ends the same as the extended ones. Screw these to the 25 × 25 mm (1 × 1 in). You may elect to have one, two or three of these in each bay, and put diagonal or square trellis infill panels, about 333 mm (13 in) deep, under the long rails, depending on how enclosed you wish to feel.

The ends of the top cross pieces may be given a pleasing shape. The collection in Fig. 2 shows how to set them out geometrically. Most of the examples here

MATERIALS

A four-bay pergola uses about as much timber as two and a half Braced Arches, plus the extra lengths of 150 × 25 mm (6 × 1 in) for the long rails, and as many strips of 75 × 25 mm (3 × 1 in) as you wish for cross-rails.

TOOLS

Cross-cut saw
Tenon saw
Jigsaw
Plane
Chisels
Drill
Screwdriver
Hammer

use a division of one-sixth of the depth of the board being worked. All have arcs scribed to start at one of these positions. Thus a two-thirds square provides striking points for more arcs.

Fig. 1

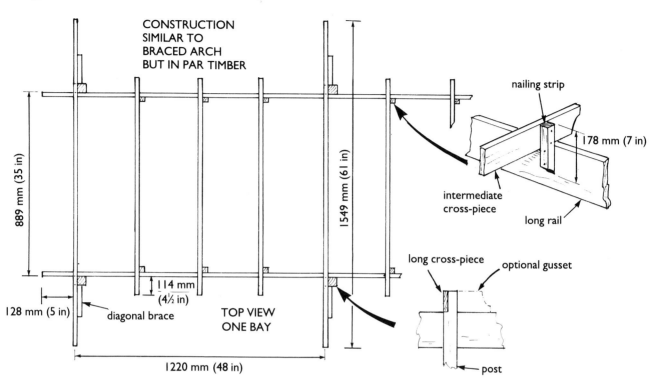

CONSTRUCTION
SIMILAR TO
BRACED ARCH
BUT IN PAR TIMBER

889 mm (35 in)

1549 mm (61 in)

114 mm (4½ in)

128 mm (5 in)

diagonal brace

TOP VIEW
ONE BAY

1220 mm (48 in)

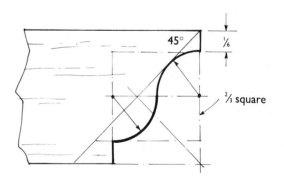

nailing strip

178 mm (7 in)

intermediate
cross-piece

long rail

long cross-piece

optional gusset

post

Fig. 2

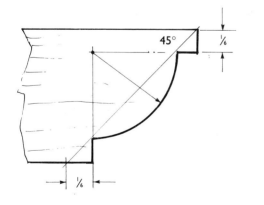

45°

⅙

⅙

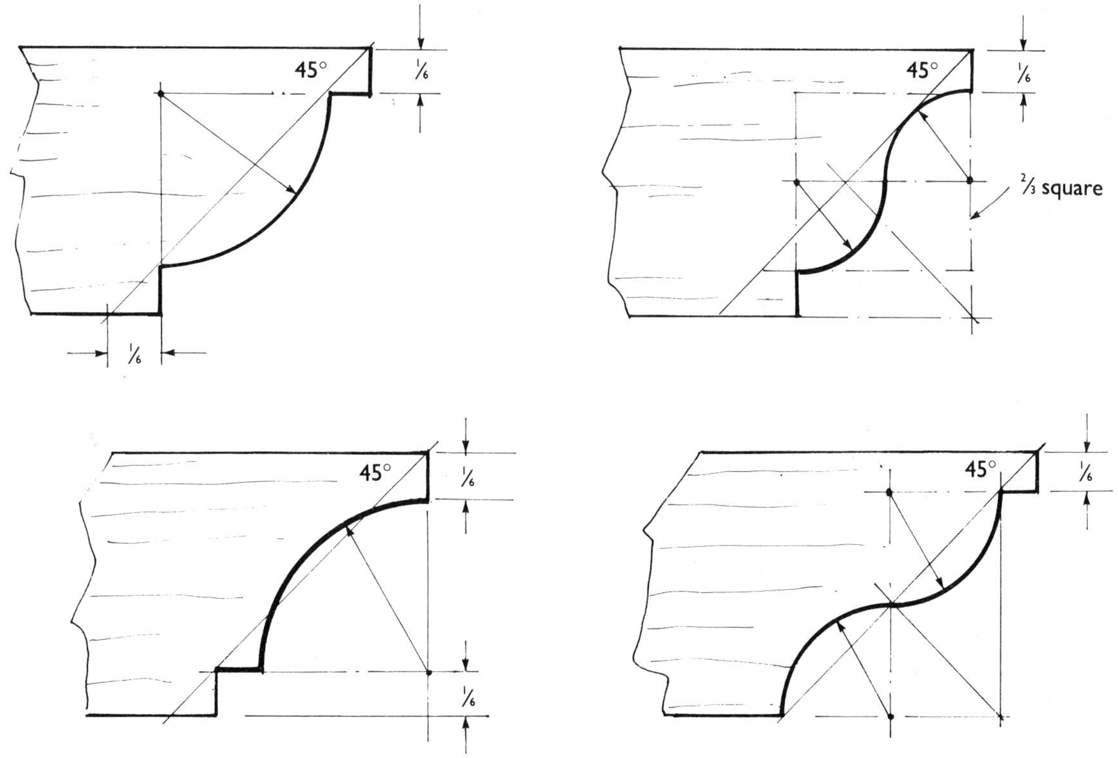

45°

⅙

⅔ square

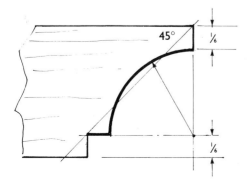

45°

⅙

⅙

45°

⅙

CURVED PERGOLA

The beauty of this pergola lies in the gentle sweep of the long box beams described.

It is no good trying to bend timber and hope that it will be held by the posts. Rather, it will try to straighten out. Therefore adopt the following strategy, using exterior ply laminations to make a box beam. It may sound complicated but you can practise with a single unit. Time yourself at the assembly stage to see if the glue will still be workable.

You can use thinner ply; 3 mm (⅛ in) is quite acceptable and it bends easily.

MATERIALS

A four-bay pergola would use the same materials as the Long Pergola, but the 150 × 25-mm (6 × 1-in) rails are replaced by one 2.5 × 1.25-metre (8 × 4-ft) sheet of 4-mm (³/₁₆-in) exterior ply and some thin battens.

TOOLS

Cross-cut and tenon saws
Circular saw
Chisels
Plane
Drill
Screwdriver
Hammer

WATCHPOINT

Choose a cool, dry day so that the glue does not 'go off' too quickly. Leave room under the bottom edge by packing it up. You can then move the 'G' cramps along easily as pins or screws hold the glued joints tight.

1 Cut pairs of 150-mm-wide (6-in) strips from a full 2.5 × 1.25-metre (8 × 4-ft) sheet of 4- or 6-mm (³⁄₁₆- or ¼-in) exterior plywood. The length of the pergola can be in units of this: 2.5, 5, 7.5 metres (8, 16, 24 ft) long.

2 With a peg and a piece of string, lay out the arc of a circle on a flat piece of lawn. Avoid too small a radius – 4.5 metres (15 ft) is quite sharp enough for the inner curve. The example shown in Fig. 1 is 5.3 metres (17 ft 2 in) to the inner curve and 6.15 metres (20 ft) to the outer rail. This turns a 5-metre (16-ft) pergola through 45 degrees.

Fig. 1

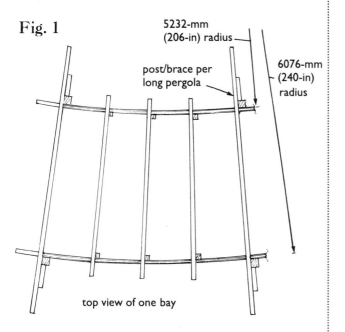

5232-mm (206-in) radius

post/brace per long pergola

6076-mm (240-in) radius

top view of one bay

3 Cut end and joiner pieces from 25 × 150 mm (1 × 6 in) and rebate them to the thickness of the plywood each side. This leaves a space between the latter to be filled with a top and bottom strip of 24-mm-deep (1-in) batten (Fig. 2). Remember that the inner rail will be shorter. You will see by how much if the curves are set out in the same relative position from a common radius point. Find the centre of the length and cut

a short strip to fit vertically where a post comes. Using weatherproof glue (epoxy or polyester resin), pin and glue both plywood strips to one end piece and allow to set. Apply glue to both sides of the top and bottom strips and place them in the space

Fig. 2

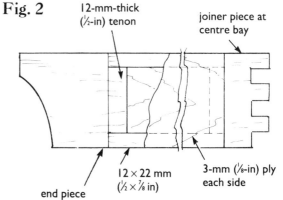

12-mm-thick (½-in) tenon

joiner piece at centre bay

12 × 22 mm (½ × ⅞ in)

3-mm (⅛-in) ply each side

end piece

between the ply outsides. Include the centre vertical spacer. Immediately pull the assembly up to a curve a little tighter than the pegs. Clamp or wedge it there until the glue sets. If any gaps show during this process, squeeze them closed with 'G' cramps and pin them. Progress along the length until all is even and tight. Fit the joiner end. Leave the job like this overnight; it should open out a little to meet the pegs. Leave it there for another day; by this time it should have set to the right curve.

Your technique may not be good enough to get perfection at the first attempt. If there is pronounced 'spring' towards straightening, tighten up the radius of the peg set-up. You will do best to attempt the tight inside curve first. This is the most testing, but when the pergola is finished it is well worth the effort.

The rest of the structure is the same as for the Long Pergola. A word of warning, though. Do not try to make things easier by sawing across the long rails to make them bend. Rather, it weakens them. The light curved box beams described are stronger than this.

Pegged Tenon Planter

CUTTING LIST				
Section		No.	Length	
mm	in		mm	in
18 × 145	$\frac{3}{4} \times 5\frac{3}{4}$	4	927	$36\frac{1}{2}$
		4	508	20
18 × 96	$\frac{3}{4} \times 3\frac{3}{4}$	1	508	20
18 × 44	$\frac{3}{4} \times 1\frac{3}{4}$	1	1524	60
		4	787	31
		2	508	20
18 × 18	$\frac{3}{4} \times \frac{3}{4}$	1	1118	44
9	$\frac{3}{8}$ ext. ply	1	280 × 787	11 × 31

TOOLS

Cross-cut and tenon saws
Jigsaw
Drill
Chisels
Screwdriver

TRADITIONALLY RUSTIC in style, this plant container has chunky pegged tusk tenons and whittled edges, yet it economizes on timber by having doubler pieces at the ends and edges. These give it strength and body. Fig. 1 shows how the basic sides, each made up from two 18 × 145-mm ($\frac{3}{4} \times 5\frac{3}{4}$-in) boards, are strengthened on the inside.

1 Cut four pieces of the widest board and, using some 18 × 44 mm ($\frac{3}{4} \times 1\frac{3}{4}$ in), mark out eight tenons, then cut them as shown in Fig. 2.

Edge-join two pieces of 18 × 145 mm ($\frac{3}{4} \times 5\frac{3}{4}$ in), using three dowels and weatherproof glue for each side panel, and cramp up with sash cramps, or rig extension strips of batten to a Workmate and use this instead (as in Fig. 3).

Fig. 1

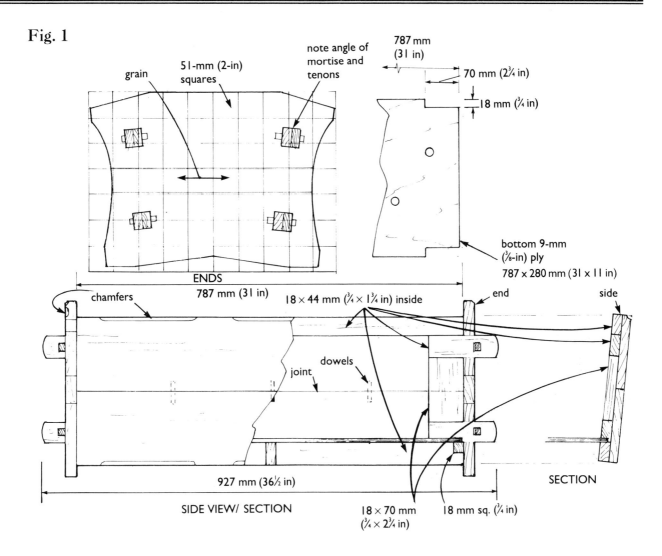

grain

51-mm (2-in) squares

note angle of mortise and tenons

787 mm (31 in)

70 mm (2¾ in)

18 mm (¾ in)

bottom 9-mm (⅜-in) ply
787 x 280 mm (31 x 11 in)

ENDS

787 mm (31 in)

18 × 44 mm (¾ × 1¾ in) inside

end

side

chamfers

joint

dowels

927 mm (36½ in)

SIDE VIEW/ SECTION

18 × 70 mm (¾ × 2¾ in)

18 mm sq. (¾ in)

SECTION

Fig. 2

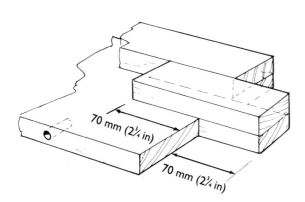

70 mm (2¾ in)

70 mm (2¾ in)

Fig. 3

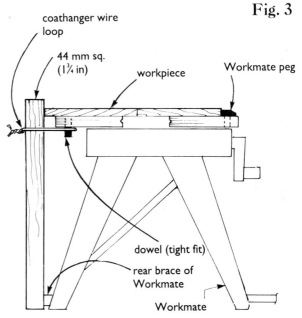

coathanger wire loop

44 mm sq. (1¾ in)

workpiece

Workmate peg

dowel (tight fit)

rear brace of Workmate

Workmate

Fig. 4

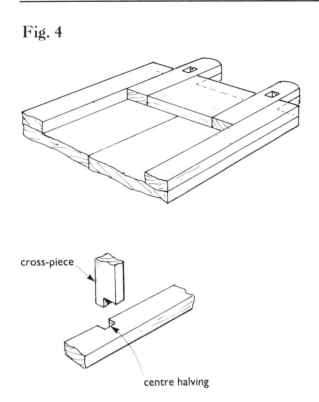

cross-piece

centre halving

Fig. 5

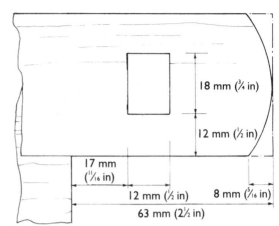

18 mm (¾ in)

12 mm (½ in)

17 mm
(¹¹⁄₁₆ in)

12 mm (½ in)   8 mm (⁵⁄₁₆ in)

63 mm (2½ in)

2 Cut pieces of 18 × 44 mm (¾ × 1¼ in) to form tenon doublers and edging strips. Cut a notch 18 × 18 mm (¾ × ¾ in) at the centre of each lower strip (Fig. 4), and glue and screw them to the glued-up side boards. Cut four pieces of 18 × 96 mm (¾ × 3¾ in) to fit tightly between the tenon doublers. Note that their grain direction is at right angles to that on the boards. This stiffens the assembly.

3 Glue and screw all these pieces to the boards. Then, when set, mark out holes for the pegs in the tenons, as in Fig. 5. Start by drilling a 12-mm (½-in) hole in each tenon, then open it out and square the corners with a chisel. As these are deep holes, you will find it much easier to attack them from both sides to get the corners neat and tidy. Then shave away any hourglass-like curve at the glue line. You could even start this opening out with a jigsaw, before finally trimming. The holes have to go right through both board and doubler parts of the tenons.

4 Cut four more pieces of the widest board and two of 18 × 44 mm (¾ × 1¾ in) to make up the width of a pair of end panels. Use four dowels to each end, plus weatherproof glue to join them. Cramp them as before, then mark out from the gridded areas on Fig. 1 the outline of the panels and the angles of the sides. Cut the outline with a jigsaw, then mark the inner faces and position the side pieces flush with the top. Angle them as described earlier, so that you can mark the angle, shape and positions of the mortises to be cut.

5 Drill and chop the mortises, checking as you go to make sure you get a good fit. They must match the angles as well as the shape. Put reference marks by the joints to ensure a quick match when gluing up. Before this happens, make four tapered pegs to drive into the holes in the tenons after they pass out through the end panels. Fig. 6 gives the proportions of these small but vital components and shows how to incorporate them accurately in the tenons.

6 This planter is deep, so there will be a heavy soil load on the floor. If the floor is not supported in the centre it might, in time, bow and pull away from the sides. Cut a piece of 18 × 44 mm (¾ × 1¾ in) to fit between the side boards at the lower edge.

Rebate it to fit the housing in the bottom rails. Glue it in place. Glue and screw strips of 18 × 18 mm (¾ × ¾ in) across inside the ends, level with the top of the bottom rails. These support the floor. Cut this from 9-mm (⅜-in) plywood, rebated around the tenon doublers so that it sits on the top of the rails. This may be left loose or screwed down. In any case, coat the top edge of the rails with weatherproof glue to seal them.

7 Using a chisel, make short chamfers on the edges of the ends and sides, as shown in Fig. 1. Work from each end so as not to cause splits in the corners. Leave them unsanded, for a hand-hewn effect. Treat the planter with preservative inside and varnish-stain or paint it outside. If you wish, the outer surfaces can be painted in contrasting colours, and edges picked out in gypsy-caravan style.

Fig. 6

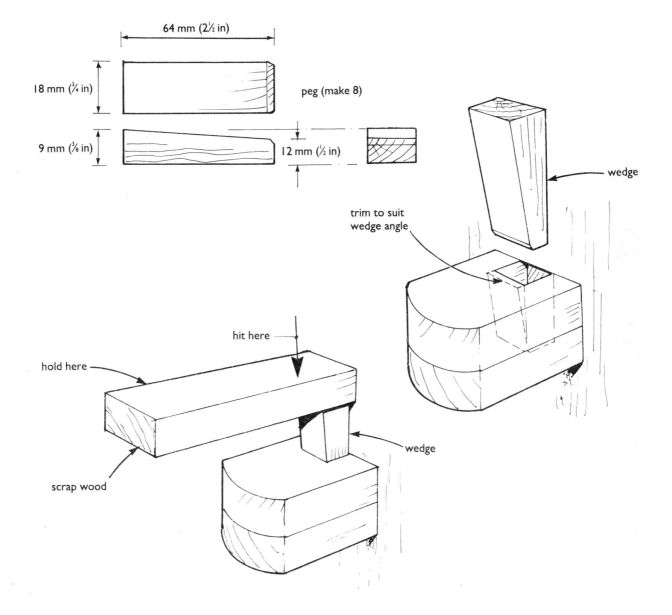

GARDEN BENCH

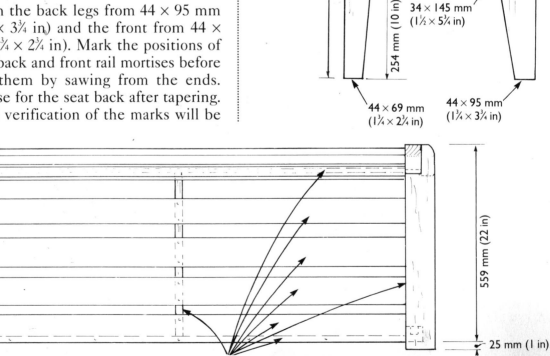

Fig. 1

stub tenon

scrap 34 mm sq (1¼ in)

rebate for front slat

686 mm (27 in)

254 mm (10 in)

34 × 145 mm (1½ × 5¾ in)

44 × 69 mm (1¼ × 2¾ in)

44 × 95 mm (1¼ × 3¾ in)

STOUT AND SIMPLE, this project is based on the traditional bench but has fewer complex joints. It seats three people and, being made in softwood, is easier to move about. Fig. 1 shows the three views.

I Form the back legs from 44 × 95 mm (1¼ × 3¾ in) and the front from 44 × 69 mm (1¼ × 2¾ in). Mark the positions of the side, back and front rail mortises before tapering them by sawing from the ends. Mark those for the seat back after tapering. The final verification of the marks will be

559 mm (22 in)

25 mm (1 in)

18 × 69 mm (¾ × 2¾ in)

Fig. 1 (cont.)

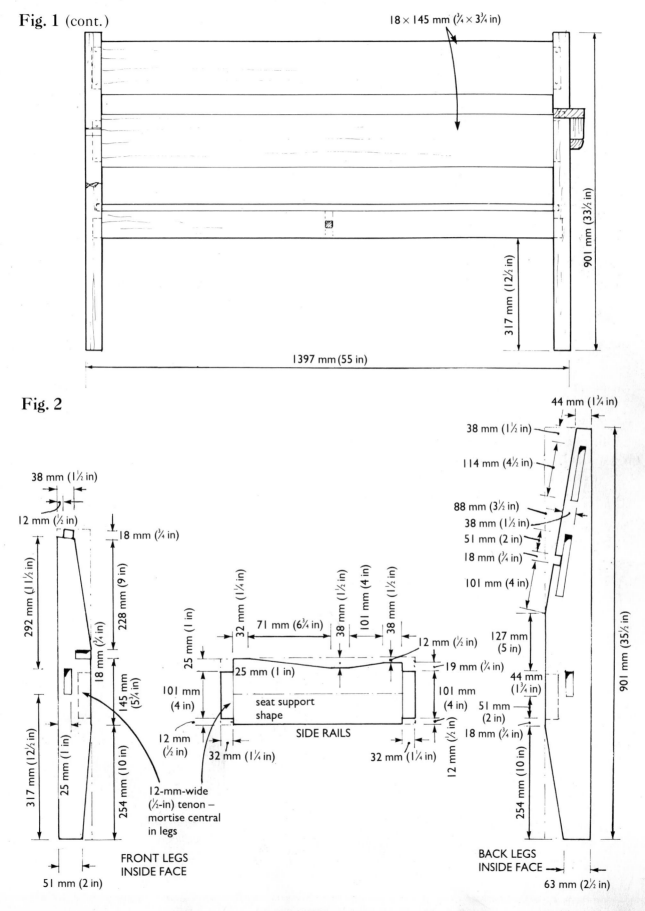

18 × 145 mm (¾ × 3¾ in)

901 mm (33½ in)

317 mm (12½ in)

1397 mm (55 in)

Fig. 2

44 mm (1¾ in)

38 mm (1½ in)

114 mm (4½ in)

88 mm (3½ in)

38 mm (1½ in)

51 mm (2 in)

18 mm (¾ in)

101 mm (4 in)

38 mm (1½ in)

12 mm (½ in)

18 mm (¾ in)

228 mm (9 in)

292 mm (11½ in)

18 mm (¾ in)

145 mm (5¾ in)

317 mm (12½ in)

25 mm (1 in)

254 mm (10 in)

12-mm-wide (½-in) tenon – mortise central in legs

FRONT LEGS INSIDE FACE

51 mm (2 in)

32 mm (1¼ in)

71 mm (6¾ in)

38 mm (1½ in)

101 mm (4 in)

38 mm (1½ in)

25 mm (1 in)

25 mm (1 in)

101 mm (4 in)

seat support shape

12 mm (½ in)

SIDE RAILS

32 mm (1¼ in)

12 mm (½ in)

19 mm (¾ in)

101 mm (4 in)

32 mm (1¼ in)

12 mm (½ in)

127 mm (5 in)

44 mm (1¾ in)

51 mm (2 in)

18 mm (¾ in)

254 mm (10 in)

901 mm (35½ in)

BACK LEGS INSIDE FACE

63 mm (2½ in)

CUTTING LIST

Section		No.	Length	
mm	in		mm	in
18 × 145	¾ × 5¾	2	1371	54
18 × 69	¾ × 2¾	6	1397	55
		2	585	23
		1	483	19
34 × 145	1½ × 5¾	2	432	17
44 × 69	1¾ × 2¾	2	686	27
44 × 95	1¾ × 3¾	2	915	36

TOOLS

Saw
Tenon saw
Jigsaw (optional)
Drill
Chisels
Router (optional)
Screwdriver
Plus usual marking and measuring
equipment

made later. Remember to have left- and right-handed versions. Also form a tenon on the top of each front leg. Saw the end rails to their top profile and trim for the depth of the tenons (see Fig. 2, which shows the mortises finished and rebates for the front seat slat and arm rest).

2 Having shaped one end rail, use it to mark the seat profile on the 18 × 69-mm (¾ × 2¾-in) seat support (Fig. 3). Make the front and back rails from more of the same section with tenons each end.

Fig. 3

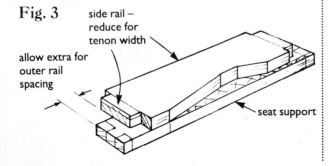

side rail – reduce for tenon width

allow extra for outer rail spacing

seat support

There is a mortise in each for the seat support (see Fig. 4). Using the sectional views in Fig. 5, reduce the tenons to width with tenon saw and chisel or with a router.

Fig. 4

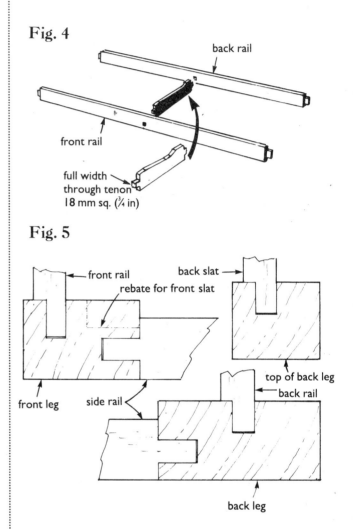

back rail

front rail

full width through tenon 18 mm sq. (¾ in)

Fig. 5

front rail

rebate for front slat

back slat

front leg

side rail

top of back leg

back rail

back leg

3 Cut the back slats to length, allowing for tenons. Shape these and reduce them on the front face only. Transfer all tenon end shapes to the mortise marks in the legs, then form the mortises with drill and chisel, or rout them if the router has enough plunge depth. Check each for fit and mark the appropriate tenon.

4 Fix the legs to the side rails with waterproof glue. Peg the joints with 6-mm (¼-in) hardwood dowels. While setting, make the arm rests from 18 × 69 mm (¾ × 2¾ in), rebated around the back legs and with a mortise marked from the front-leg tenon – a left- and right-handed pair.

5 Dry-assemble in the following order. Prop one end frame against the wall on its back. Insert both back slats, then rebate out. Then the back rail. Insert the seat support, and add the front rail, which will now be supported.

Place the other end on its back, close to the end of the top back slat. Guide the corner of this in first. Swing the legs in progressively as the next slat and back rail go in. Bring the side up vertical as the front rail goes in. If all fits properly, disassemble and glue up. Take a rope around the rails and apply pressure by using a stick as a tourniquet. Do the same with the seat back. Check for squareness in plan view.

6 Cut the seat slats to length. Notch the front one to fit partly around the front legs and partly in the rebates in them. Glue and screw it to the front rail and centre

support. Glue and screw the remaining slats in place.

Now glue the arms in place, and add reinforcing blocks screwed to the back legs. Finally peg the front and back rails and trim the peg ends (carefully, because they are harder than the main woodwork).

Sand, fill and varnish to suit the location.

7 Have you ever tried to site a garden bench near a bank? Making a neat job of it involves much excavation and wall-building (as in Fig. 6). Often, rubbish then collects in the recess you have created.

If the bank is a convenient height it can support the rear of the seat on walling slabs. Simply cut the back legs to suit, as in Fig. 7. You save space and work, but remember that seats with leg stretchers lose strength. This project should be strong enough, or you may like to design a bench with extended seat rails to reach far back.

Fig. 6

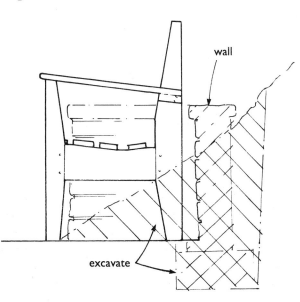

wall / excavate

Fig. 7

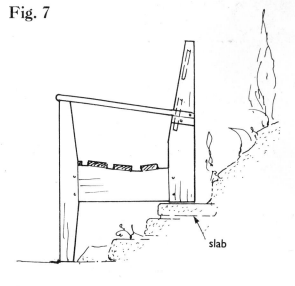

slab

GAZEBO

THE GAZEBO provides you with a spot to sit and frame the view. It is not intended to be weatherproof – that is the job of a summer house.

Gazebos are decorative from outside and inside, so this one has trellis around the open gabled front. It has a floor and integral seat, and partly open sides, which can be covered by hinged screens to cut out draughts. The roof is a series of open rafters, to give the effect of a small pergola. Fig. 1 shows the front and side elevations, floor and section. You can make it in sections and assemble it on a completely level base made from slabs or bricks to project just past the edges. Provided the ground has been levelled and cleared of grass and weeds, the gazebo can sit on small blocks at all the frame joints, to allow ventilation underneath so as to avoid dry rot. In windy areas, provide long metal spikes to anchor it down to concrete blocks.

Fig. 1

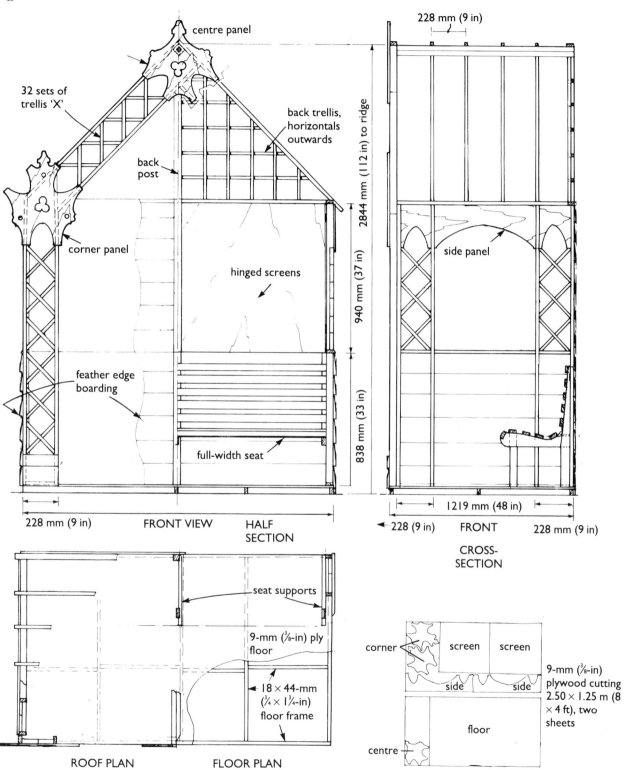

centre panel

32 sets of
trellis 'X'

back trellis,
horizontals
outwards

back
post

corner panel

hinged screens

feather edge
boarding

full-width seat

2844 mm (112 in) to ridge

940 mm (37 in)

838 mm (33 in)

228 mm (9 in)

FRONT VIEW

HALF
SECTION

228 mm (9 in)

side panel

1219 mm (48 in)

228 (9 in)

FRONT
CROSS-
SECTION

228 mm (9 in)

seat supports

9-mm (³⁄₈-in) ply
floor

18 × 44-mm
(³⁄₄ × 1³⁄₄-in)
floor frame

ROOF PLAN

FLOOR PLAN

corner

screen   screen

side   side

centre

floor

9-mm (³⁄₈-in)
plywood cutting
2.50 × 1.25 m (8
× 4 ft), two
sheets

Fig. 2

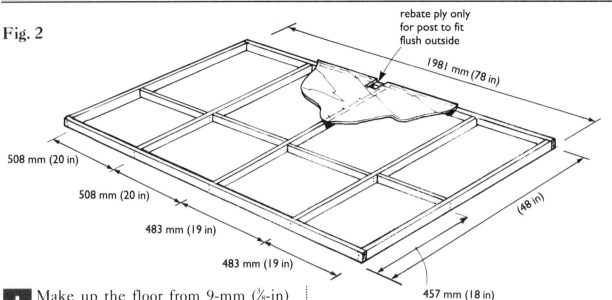

rebate ply only for post to fit flush outside

1981 mm (78 in)

508 mm (20 in)

508 mm (20 in)

483 mm (19 in)

483 mm (19 in)

(48 in)

457 mm (18 in)

1 Make up the floor from 9-mm (⅜-in) exterior ply on a frame of 18 × 44 mm ¾ × 1¾ in) (Fig. 2). This is a complete unit which will fit to the sides, back and front later. Form a rebate for the centre back post.

CUTTING LIST					
Section		**No.**	**Length**		
mm	in		m/mm	ft/in	
44 × 44	1¾ × 1¾	1	2794	110	
		1	1219	48	
18 × 69	¾ × 2¾	3	762	30	
		3	457	18	
18 × 44	¾ × 1¾	6	2006	79	
		10	1930	76	
		10	1829	72	
		4	1514	60	
		2	1346	53	
		11	1219	48	
		2	190	7½	
18 × 18	¾ × ¾		60 m	195 ft	
			for trellis and roof		
Feather edge					
152	6	13	2007	79	
		12	1219	48	
		2	228	9	
9	⅜ ext. ply	2	2.5 × 1.25 m	8 × 4 ft	

Fig. 3

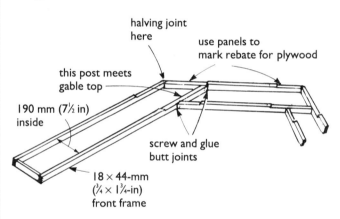

halving joint here

use panels to mark rebate for plywood

this post meets gable top

190 mm (7½ in) inside

screw and glue butt joints

18 × 44-mm (¾ × 1¾-in) front frame

2 Using 18 × 44 mm (¾ × 1¾ in), make up the front frame complete with gable, using halving joints. The wood is on edge for both inner and outer parts. Rebate for the corner joiner panels (Fig. 3).

TOOLS
Cross-cut and tenon saws
Jigsaw
Plane
Chisels
Drill
Screwdrivers
Hammer
Router (optional)

Fig. 4

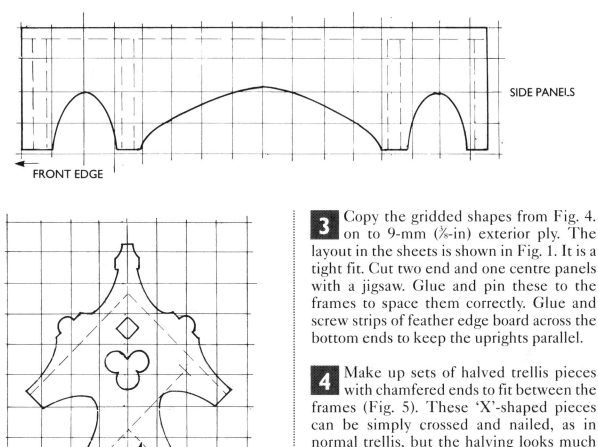

SIDE PANELS

← FRONT EDGE

76 mm (3 in)
squares

CENTRE
PANEL

mark positions
of frames on
back

← outside edge   END PANELS

3 Copy the gridded shapes from Fig. 4. on to 9-mm (⅜-in) exterior ply. The layout in the sheets is shown in Fig. 1. It is a tight fit. Cut two end and one centre panels with a jigsaw. Glue and pin these to the frames to space them correctly. Glue and screw strips of feather edge board across the bottom ends to keep the uprights parallel.

4 Make up sets of halved trellis pieces with chamfered ends to fit between the frames (Fig. 5). These 'X'-shaped pieces can be simply crossed and nailed, as in normal trellis, but the halving looks much neater. Make sure, however, that the chamfered faces of all the 'X'-shaped pieces fit exactly between the verticals and the gable strips.

Fig. 5

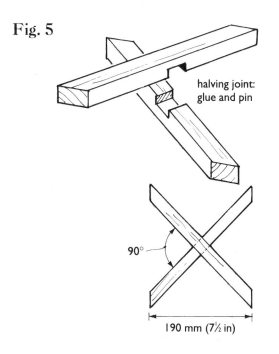

halving joint:
glue and pin

90°

190 mm (7½ in)

5 Lay the frame, panel-side down, and glue and pin the trellis pieces in flush with the front edge. This completes the front.

6 Make up two side frames with more 18 × 44 mm (¾ × 1¾ in) on edge, but board up to sill line outside with horizontal feather edge board. Use thin nails near the edge of the boards, and make sure that they do not split the frame work or pass through where their points will show.

Cut two side panels from 9-mm (⅜-in) plywood and glue and pin them at the top edge. They are not set in rebates. Fill in the narrow panels at each end with more halved trellis pieces, flush outside.

7 Make a back gable frame from 18 × 44 mm (¾ × 1¾ in), halved to a central post of 44 × 44 mm (1¾ × 1¾ in) (Fig. 6).

Fig. 6

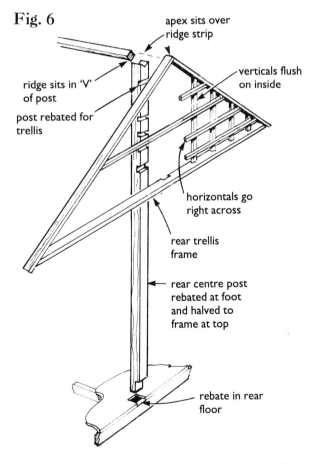

apex sits over ridge strip

ridge sits in 'V' of post

post rebated for trellis

verticals flush on inside

horizontals go right across

rear trellis frame

rear centre post rebated at foot and halved to frame at top

rebate in rear floor

Watch the joint – it is weak at this stage. The gable bottom has to be level with the top of the gazebo sides. Fill in the top of the gable

with 18 × 18-mm (¾ × ¾-in) trellis, not halved this time but with the verticals flush on the outside and the horizontals flush on the inside, and let into rebates in the post.

8 Lay the front frame face down, screw the floor to it and clamp the gazebo sides to the back of the frame. Screw them to the floor and top of the front frame.

Tip the construction right way up and continue screwing the sides to the front. Stand the back post central and drop its rebated end into the rebate in the floor. Screw the post to the floor frame. Screw the gable ends to the sides, where it sits on top.

Now fill in the back up to the gable with feather edge boarding and fix each board to the side uprights. This now completes the back.

9 Screw the 44 × 44-mm (1¾ × 1¾-in) ridge piece between front and back gables. Rebate the front end to fit into the front ply panel. Insert the screws through the frames into the ridge.

Add 18 × 18-mm (¾ × ¾-in) 'rafter' strips from ridge to the top of the side frames, overlap this by 44 mm (1¾ in) over the frame top.

10 Shape supports for the seat and its back from 18 × 69 mm (¾ × 2¾ in), as in Fig. 7. There are three pairs. Screw these to the side walls, and a central one to one

Fig. 7

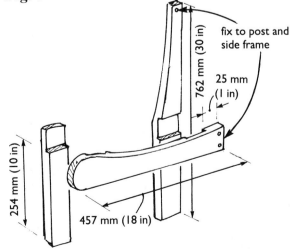

762 mm (30 in)

fix to post and side frame

25 mm (1 in)

254 mm (10 in)

457 mm (18 in)

side of the central upright at the back wall. Cover the seat and back with 18 × 44-mm (¾ × 1¾-in) slats spaced 25 mm (1 in) apart (gaps, not centres!). Round off the edges near the front.

█ Cut two panels from the remaining 9-mm (⅜-in) plywood to fit between the back corners and the centre post. Hinge them to each of the back-corner uprights so that they fold out across the central opening each side. Fit wood turn-buttons to hold them to the side-trellis uprights or to the centre back post when folded in.

FINISHING

The underside of the floor and its frame should be treated with preservative to resist rot, but the rest, inside and out, may be treated with a light or clear finish to preserve the woody appearance. Painting the thing white is a fiddly job, with all the trellis, so you may wish to opt for natural-looking preservative stain finish. Perhaps the back wall and seat could be a different shade, but do try to make the plywood parts match the rest. This will mean shading the pine towards the warm tones. The whole thing would look fussy if the ply was picked out in a different tone deliberately.

The feather edge boards are sawn-finish, so opt for a matt preservative stain rather than varnish. Here you have a contrast if you are going to paint the rest. If you can afford it, shiplap boarding is an alternative to the feather edge, but it makes the whole thing heavier.

Remember to have hold-down pegs or stakes if the gazebo is in a windy location. Even the openwork style of this project will catch the wind if it blows from the front . . . Has anyone seen a low-flying gazebo? Yes, they migrate about this time!

If you live in a damp or chilly area you might like to add a solid roof over the trellis strips and cover the rear gable outside to keep rain out. The hinged sides do this already.

Feather edge board looks quite in keeping with the other parts clad in this material. The roof panels can be made removable for the hot summers. Fit the boards to 18 × 44-mm (¾ × 1¾-in) strips spaced to sit edge to edge with the front and rear gable strips. The feather edge will overlap the latter and removable screws or bolts will hold it (Fig. 8).

Fig. 8

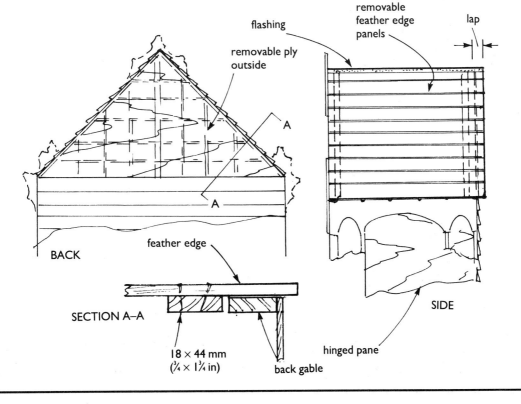

TREE SEAT (FOR A BORDER TREE)

SOMETIMES A GARDEN has just the right type of tree to build a seat around but it unfortunately grows too close to a hedge or boundary.

Rather than feeling you have to discard the idea, simply make the seat fit just part of the way round. A strut behind the tree makes the ends stable, and the size can be chosen to suit the job. Naturally it requires less timber and time, because there are two main units and a bridging piece. If at any time it is to be moved to an 'all-round' site, one more unit and two more bridge pieces complete the hexagon. Fig. 1 shows the three-piece job.

The siting of the ideal shape is shown in Fig. 2. Note how the border-side path is extended back on each side, and the straight joiner strut is hidden near the fence. Compare this with Fig. 3, which shows the distance required between a boundary and a tree for the full hexagon. Who wants to face a blank view, anyway?

It goes without saying that the space in the 'half' version is wider than it is deep, but in years to come the seat may be moved outwards and the straight strut joiner replaced with an angled one, as in Fig. 4. Just because there is a change of angle in this strut, it does not mean that it will not provide enough rigidity. Each end of the strut is screwed to the seat bearers in two places. This acts as a stabilizing lever to control rock, rather than angular spread.

Fig. 1

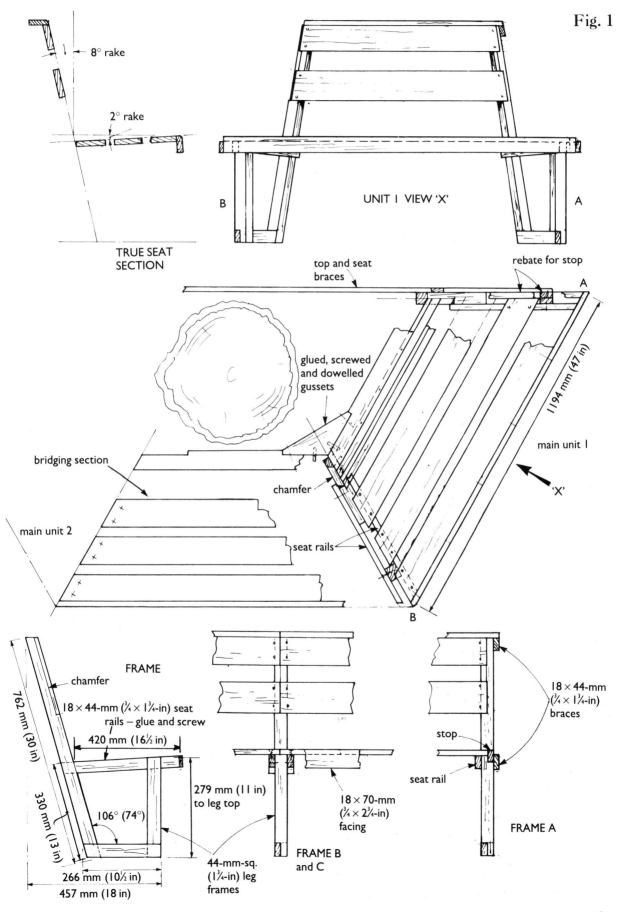

8° rake

2° rake

TRUE SEAT
SECTION

UNIT I VIEW 'X'

B

A

top and seat
braces

rebate for stop

A

glued, screwed
and dowelled
gussets

1194 mm (47 in)

bridging section

main unit I

chamfer

'X'

main unit 2

seat rails

B

FRAME

chamfer

18 × 44-mm (¾ × 1¼-in) seat
rails – glue and screw

420 mm (16½ in)

762 mm (30 in)

330 mm (13 in)

106° (74°)

266 mm (10½ in)

457 mm (18 in)

279 mm (11 in)
to leg top

18 × 70-mm
(¾ × 2¾-in)
facing

44-mm-sq.
(1¾-in) leg
frames

FRAME B
and C

18 × 44-mm
(¾ × 1¼-in)
braces

stop

seat rail

FRAME A

Fig. 2

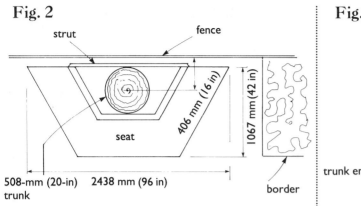

strut

fence

seat

406 mm (16 in)

1067 mm (42 in)

border

508-mm (20-in) trunk

2438 mm (96 in)

Fig. 4

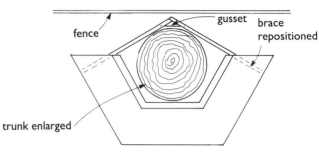

fence

gusset

brace repositioned

trunk enlarged

Fig. 3

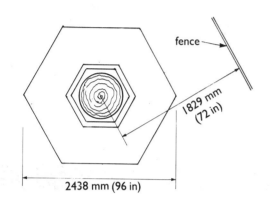

fence

1829 mm (72 in)

2438 mm (96 in)

Mark out on a scrap piece of hardboard or ply the pattern for the basic leg frame, as in Fig. 1. Lay 44 × 44 mm (1¾ × 1¾ in) over it and mark lengths and angles of the halving joints. Cut chamfers for the seat back on the longest strips (Fig. 5). Two have double chamfers, and one each has a single chamfer. Do one left- and one right-handed, all at 30 degrees, not forgetting to cut the top and bottom chamfers on each end and the halving at the same angle.

Fig. 5

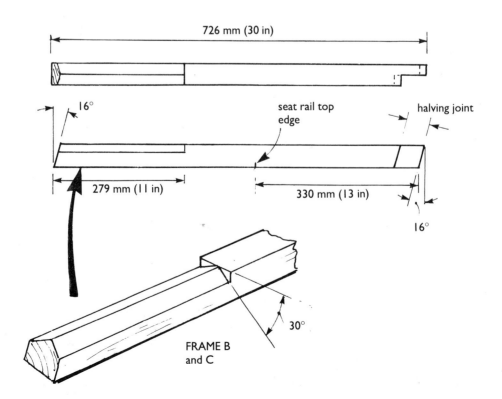

726 mm (30 in)

16°

seat rail top edge

halving joint

279 mm (11 in)

330 mm (13 in)

16°

30°

FRAME B and C

2 Glue and screw the frames to produce four 'J'-shaped units. Screw and glue a pair of 18 × 44-mm (¾ × 1¾-in) strips to join front to back, making a bearer for the seat slats. Note the slightly raked angle. The double chamfered frames need one bearer each side, as in Fig. 6; the other two have one each on the chamfered side.

Fig. 6

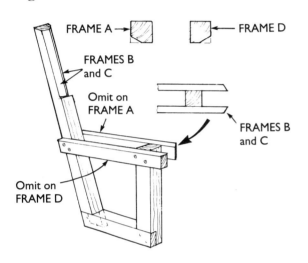

FRAME A →

← FRAME D

FRAMES B and C

Omit on FRAME A

FRAMES B and C

Omit on FRAME D

3 All the seat and back slats are 18 × 95 mm (¾ × 3¾ in). Carefully mark and cut each end of the front set of seat slats to 29.5 degrees. This is to allow for the difference in angle from the 30-degree joints produced by the slight rake on the seat. If the seat was dead flat, then a 30-degree angle would fit.

You can take one frame with two bearers and one end frame, and set them up on a flat floor. Check that the frames stand upright and tack a couple of waste battens across to hold them, as in Fig. 7.

Measure across the tops of the back pieces. This will give you the length of the top back slat. These need to be chamfered both at 10 degrees on the face, to allow for the back slope, and at 30 degrees on the end, to meet each other. Fig. 8 (overleaf) explains. You may find it more accurate first to cut the end angle, then chamfer this cut, rather than angle sawing both together.

CUTTING LIST					
Section		**No.**	**Length**		
mm	in		mm	in	
18 × 95	¾ × 3¾	3	1219	48	
		3	1067	42	
		3	889	35	
		3	736	29	
		3	660	26	
		1	457	18	
18 × 70	¾ × 2¾	3	1219	48	
		3	686	27	
44 × 44	1¾ × 1¾	3	762	30	
		3	330	13	
		3	279	11	
18 × 44	¾ × 1¾	1	2438	96	
		1	711	28	
		8	432	17	

TOOLS
Cross-cut saw
Tenon saw
Chisels
Plane
Drill
Screwdriver
Adjustable square
Spirit level

Fig. 7

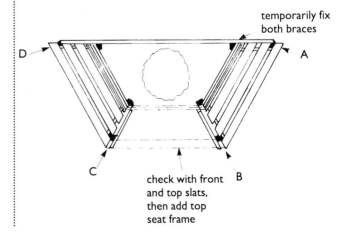

temporarily fix both braces

D

A

check with front and top slats, then add top seat frame

C

B

Fig. 8

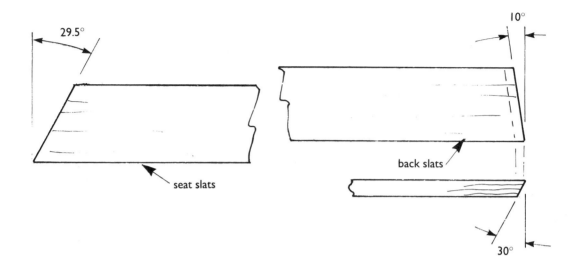

seat slats

back slats

4 Assemble these frames with the first front seat slat and the top back slat, using screws only. Now measure the lengths required for the centre and rear seat slat and the lower back slat. Select these from the cutting list. If you scribe these, you will also have the angles marked.

Now comes the easy bit.

5 Measure two sets of slats and cut them to shape. Assemble a second mirror-image of the first one. Place this relative to the first, as in Fig. 7 (imagine the tree). Lay the remaining slats on the seat rails and hold the back slats in place to check the effect and the fit. If all is well, cut a set of top caps from 18 × 70 mm (¾ × 2¾ in), all chamfered at 30 degrees. Rebate them for joiner triangles, measured from Fig. 1. Dowel and glue this set together to form a rigid frame.

6 If all fitted correctly, you can unscrew the slats and refit with glue as well.

Now to the garden . . . Position the two assembled units at the tree and check that they are spaced correctly. Use one front slat for this. Lay the top frame over the seat back to check the angles. Mark the position of the frames where they rest on the ground. Drive pegs in to mark them. It is unlikely that it will stand straight, so move the parts away and form level areas for each foot, as in Fig. 9. Pieces of small paving slabs or large

quarry tiles will do. Check that these are level with each other and level towards front and back, then assemble the three units together in position.

7 Cut three facing slats for the seat. Glue and screw them to the edge to strengthen the slat. Glue and screw the top cap to the top of the back slats and to the frame tops, and sand off any sharpness at the outer corners. When thoroughly set, move the seat away from the tree enough to reach the back (this takes two people). Apply preservative stain or varnish stain. Drill the end frames for bolts near the seat and measure for the joiner strut, which can also be coated with preservative.

Finally, reposition the seat and bolt the joiner in place behind the tree. Reach under the seat to do this.

Fig. 9

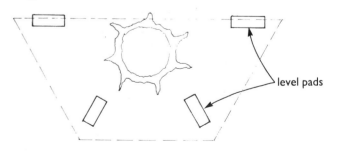

level pads

GARDENER'S TRUNDLE SEAT

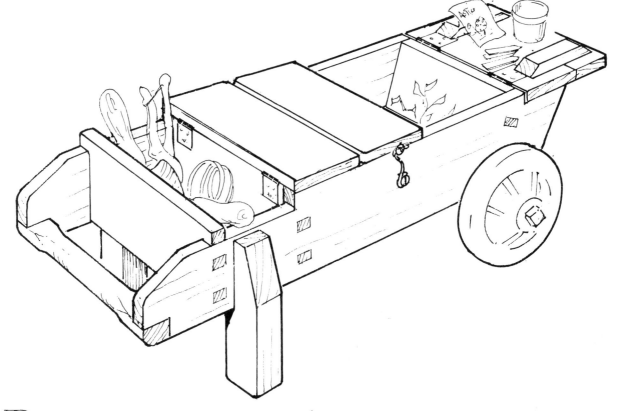

DO YOU NORMALLY struggle round the garden weighed down with bucket, stool, tools, barrow, plants and so on? Well, now you can take it easy. Sit down to that spot of weeding with the Trundle Seat. It can be wheeled around the narrow paths a barrow cannot manage, and will carry all your weeding rubbish, or plants and small hand-tools like trowels, forks and dibbers. The lid forms a seat, and part-opens to serve as a shelf for seed trays and pots.

Figs. 1–9 give a clear idea of the various permutations.

As a light barrow (Fig. 1), it can transport loose rubbish. With the lid closed – if the tool compartment is open – nothing can blow away.

Fig. 2 shows the Trundle Seat at work – a wide, low seat for weeding, with a hole through which to pop weeds into the box.

Fig. 3 shows how to access the tool area, which also extends the seat.

One of the seat boards can be used as something to kneel on in the flower bed, while still retaining both seat and access area (Fig. 4).

Open the front area and you have a cantilevered shelf and full box access, plus the kneeler (Fig. 5).

When the tool lid is open, it does not restrict much of the box access (Fig. 6). The shelf is not intended for sitting on when open.

Fig. 7 shows the Trundle Seat as in the sketch at the top of this page, with access to tools and box, and a seat and shelf in use.

When dumping rubbish, tip it into a tray, so that it can be handled easily. The shelf acts as a guide over which to scrape the bits (Fig. 8).

Although small, some bags of material may be inconvenient to heave into a wheelbarrow. Fig. 9 shows how the shelf acts as a ramp while the bag is slid into the box. The front ends of the box sides rest on the ground to steady it.

The construction introduces simple through mortise and tenon joints. You will need a pair of 180-mm (7-in) nylon trolley wheels from the DIY shop. The drawing in Fig. 10 shows the side and top view, plus a couple of sections. The whole thing may be made larger, but watch the widths or it may not negotiate your narrowest path.

Fig. 1

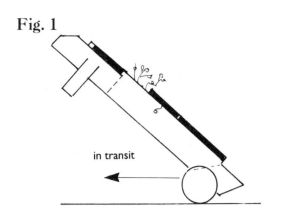

in transit

Fig. 2

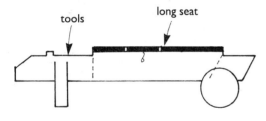

access

seat

Fig. 3

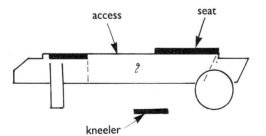

tools

long seat

Fig. 4

access

seat

kneeler

Fig. 5

full access

shelf

kneeler

Fig. 6

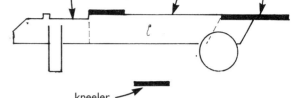

tools

open

shelf

kneeler

Fig. 7

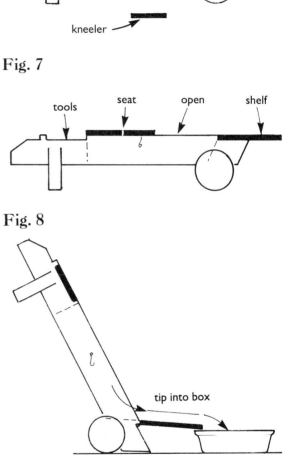

tools

seat

open

shelf

Fig. 8

tip into box

Fig. 9

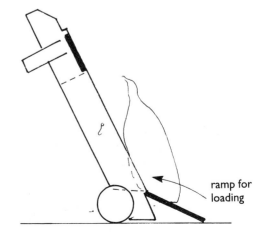

ramp for
loading

Fig. 10

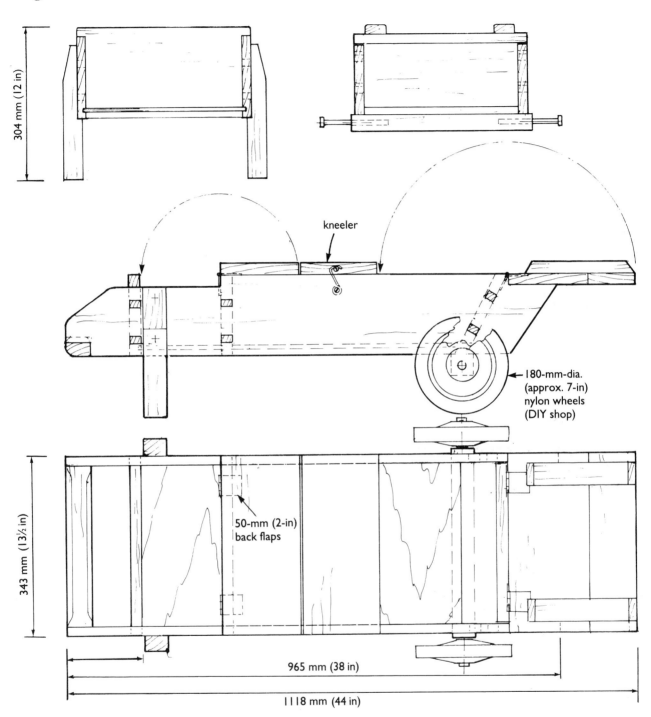

304 mm (12 in)

kneeler

180-mm-dia. (approx. 7-in) nylon wheels (DIY shop)

50-mm (2-in) back flaps

343 mm (13½ in)

965 mm (38 in)

1118 mm (44 in)

The box has 18 × 145-mm (¾ × 5¾-in) sides into which are tenoned the ends and partition. It has a 6-mm (¼-in) ply bottom, which is glued and screwed into rebates along the sides and back. The lids are also 18 × 145 mm (¾ × 5¾ in) and a 18 × 96 mm (¾ × 3¾ in). The 44 × 44-mm (1¾ × 1¾-in) legs and axle beams are screwed and glued to the box, and a handle is fixed with a halving joint to the sides.

There may be readers who forget the tenons and simply knock the thing together with screws or even nails, but as presented here the trundle seat should last much longer. . . Besides, woodwork should be a joy rather than a chore.

Fig. 11

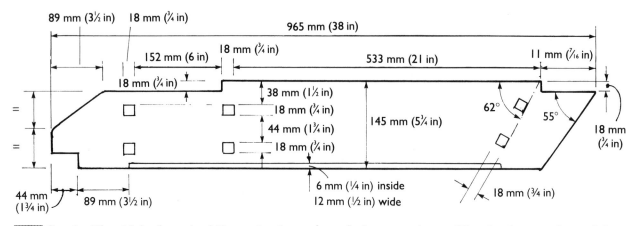

1 Study Fig. 10 before deciding whether to vary things to suit your particular requirements. Mark out and cut the outline of the sides, as in Fig. 11. Check that the wood thickness is 18 mm (¾ in). This controls the recesses for the lids and the size of the mortises. Check the angles with a sliding bevel, or make a card template.

2 Mark out the wood to the overall sizes of the front, back and partition, as in Fig. 12. Do not mark or cut the tenons yet.

Fig. 12

Fig. 13

Fig. 14

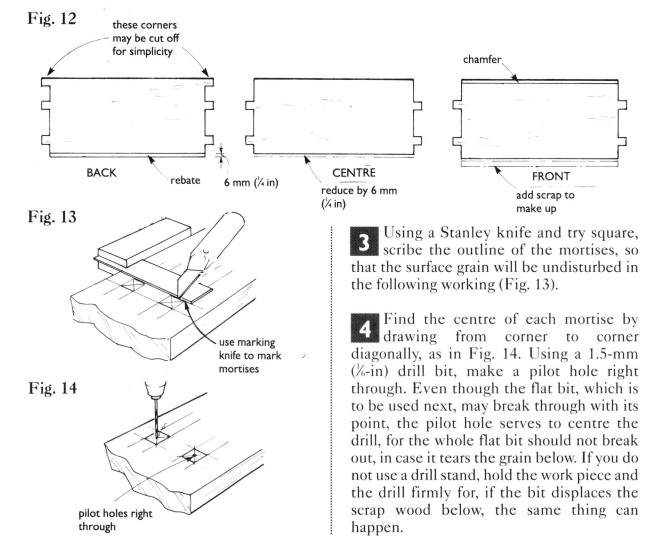

3 Using a Stanley knife and try square, scribe the outline of the mortises, so that the surface grain will be undisturbed in the following working (Fig. 13).

4 Find the centre of each mortise by drawing from corner to corner diagonally, as in Fig. 14. Using a 1.5-mm (⅙-in) drill bit, make a pilot hole right through. Even though the flat bit, which is to be used next, may break through with its point, the pilot hole serves to centre the drill, for the whole flat bit should not break out, in case it tears the grain below. If you do not use a drill stand, hold the work piece and the drill firmly for, if the bit displaces the scrap wood below, the same thing can happen.

5 Mark the flat bit with a piece of masking tape so that you will be able to judge when the main blade has gone half-way through the wood, as in Fig. 15. Just a tweak of the drill trigger should take it that far. There are twelve such cuts to make. Turn the wood over and attack it from the back to make clean-through holes.

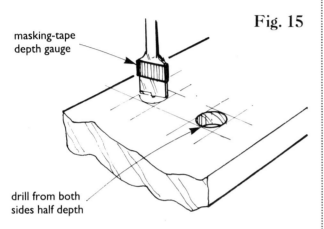

Fig. 15

masking-tape depth gauge

drill from both sides half depth

6 Rest the side piece on a scrap of wood so that the chisel edge, which will now be used, or the bench does not suffer. Use a 18-mm (¾-in) chisel, as in Fig. 16. Cut down across the grain in gentle stages from front and back, turning the round holes into square ones to match the thickness of the wood.

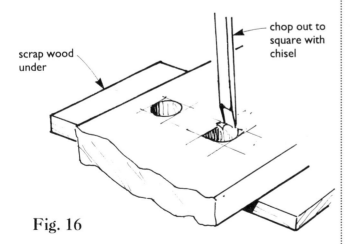

chop out to square with chisel

scrap wood under

Fig. 16

7 Lay the front, back and partition pieces on the sides and scribe the positions of the mortises to their ends and faces, as in Fig. 17. Remember that the front is angled and will be chamfered, so mark it, and the sides, for register.

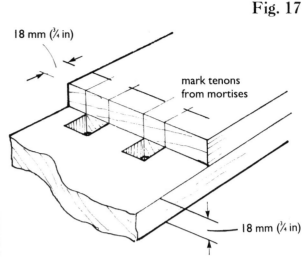

Fig. 17

18 mm (¾ in)

mark tenons from mortises

18 mm (¾ in)

8 So that the sides will not be accidentally transposed, and to form a seating for the bottom plywood, cut a rebate to the inner bottom edge. This could be run the full length with a rebate plane, but is neater if stopped, as in Fig. 18. A router is ideal for this job; otherwise mark and chisel it out. Be sure to make a left- and right-handed pair of sides.

Fig. 18

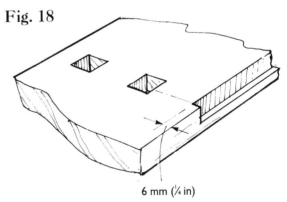

6 mm (¼ in)

9 Cut the tenons on the waste side of the marked lines. To avoid mistakes, scribble with pencil on those waste areas. Start cutting with a tenon saw from the edge of the wood towards the end, as in Fig. 19. Continue down, levelling the saw to 90 degrees as you reach the corner next to the other guideline (Fig. 20). The outer pieces of the ends can also be sawn to meet the tenon, forming a notch at the corner. If you do this it will greatly reduce the working time on the twelve corners of the ends and on the partition pieces.

Fig. 19

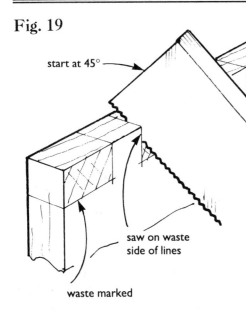

start at 45°

saw on waste side of lines

waste marked

Fig. 20

90°

10 You could use a coping saw to remove the central waste after the rest of the tenon-saw work is done, but this entails careful following of the guideline. If you have a power hand-jigsaw, it is easier (see Fig. 21). Drill a couple of 4.5-mm (³/₁₆-in) holes close together to make a small slot for starting the jigsaw blade, then cut freehand up to the tenons from both directions.

Fig. 21

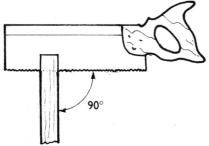

drill to admit jigsaw

saw to gauge line

To be really accurate about it, clamp a piece of batten across to guide the foot of the jigsaw, as in Fig. 22. The blade should be in the centre of its foot, so cuts can be made from both directions up to the tenons.

Fig. 22

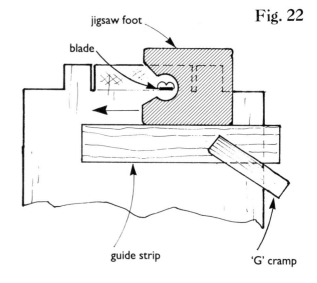

jigsaw foot

blade

guide strip

'G' cramp

Do make sure, however, that the foot, if adjustable for tilt, is at 90 degrees to the blade side.

11 Check that all the tenons fit in their mortises. If necessary, shave them so they fit well but are not sloppy. Using waterproof glue on the ends and tenons, fix to the sides. Cut the bottom to fit snugly and use it to align the box for squareness. Place the job on its side on a level surface and put weights on it.

12 When set, plane a piece of 18 × 18 mm (¾ × ¾ in) to a wedge-shaped cross-section and try it for fit between the bottom of the front piece and the plywood bottom. Glue and screw the bottom in place and follow up with the axle beam, which is a 380-mm (15-in) length of 44 × 44 mm (1¾ × 1¾ in). Cut, notch and chamfer the legs (more 44 × 44 mm), and glue and screw them to the sides from the inside.

13 Use a strip of 33 × 44 mm (1¼ × 1¾ in) for the handle. Notch the top edges 12 mm (½ in) to be 'halved' into the sides. Screw, glue and screw from below. Round off the corners where the hands will grip. Do not go right up to the sides.

14 Cut all the top pieces for the seat/lids to the outside width of the box – or fractionally wider, to allow cold fingers to grip. Edge-glue a 18 × 96 mm (¾ × 3¾ in) to

CUTTING LIST

Section		No.	Length	
mm	in		mm	in
18 × 145	¾ × 5¾	2	965	38
		6	343	13½
18 × 96	¾ × 3¾	1	343	13½
44 × 44	1¾ × 1¾	1	368	14½
		2	250	10
33 × 44	1¼ × 1¾	1	343	13½
18 × 18	¾ × ¾	1	303	12
12 × 44	½ × 1¾	2	154	6
6	¼ ext. ply	1	365 × 500	13 × 20

TOOLS

Cross-cut, tenon and coping saws
Electric drill and drill bits, including flat bits
Screwdriver
Rebate plane (or router)
18-mm (¾-in) chisel
Carpenter's square and bevel
Portable electric circular saw (optional)
Electric jigsaw (in place of coping saw – optional)
Router (optional)

one 18 × 145-mm (¾ × 5¾-in) board. These form the shelf/lid. Then glue and screw two strips of 12 × 44 mm (½ × 1¾ in) on to the top surface of the shelf to stiffen it. Chamfer the ends of these strips when set.

15 Put a No. 8 roundhead woodscrew into each end of the board to be used as a kneeler. Make a pair of hooks from 12 g fence wire and pivot them on two more roundhead No. 8s in the sides. These will secure the board in transit.

16 Recess pairs of 51-mm (2-in) steel butt hinges flush in the front top edge when it has been planed level with the sides. Cut corresponding recesses in the face of the shelf when the stiffeners are uppermost. Hinge the toolbox lid to the partition top when it is closed over the toolbox.

17 Use two 150-mm-long (6-in) steel bolts to fit the wheels. Alternatively, cut lengths of screwed rod, fit nuts and epoxy them firmly on. Epoxy the threads to make a smooth running surface, but check that the wheels move freely after it has set. Drill the axle beam to take bolts or rods undersize, so that they cut a thread in the wood. Put a washer between the wheels and the ends of the axle beam. See Fig. 23.

Fig. 23

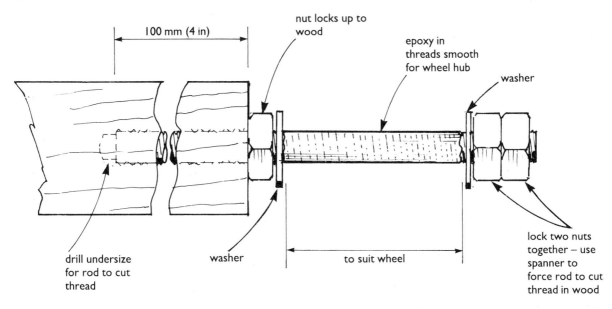

100 mm (4 in)

nut locks up to wood

epoxy in threads smooth for wheel hub

washer

drill undersize for rod to cut thread

washer

to suit wheel

lock two nuts together – use spanner to force rod to cut thread in wood

TECHNICAL TIPS

Fig. 2

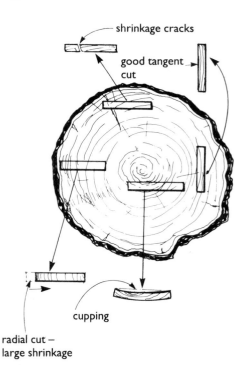

CHOOSING WOOD

Pine (deal, Norway spruce, Scots pine, Baltic pine) to be found at most woodyards and DIY shops has been checked for the more noticeable defects as part of the sizing and handling stages before you see it. Happily, few if any companies offer wood of this type from non-sustainable sources.

What you will need to look at carefully, however, is the position of knots or irregular grain near where you want to place a joint or fixing, in areas that will be shaped, and on small-cross-section material, where they will weaken its resistance to bending. Fig. 1 shows a collection of unwanted faults in strategic places.

Fig. 1

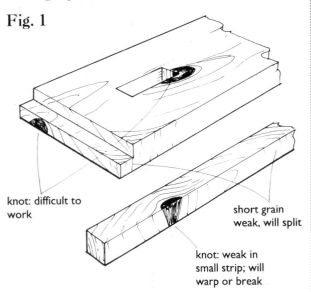

knot: difficult to work

short grain weak, will split

knot: weak in small strip; will warp or break

Watch for a tendency to warp. The part of the tree from which the wood was taken will determine how cut wood behaves.

Boards are most likely to suffer if they are cut from trees which had a small trunk diameter, because there will be a great change in the grain pattern. Similarly, boards are not usually cut from the centre of the tree (the heartwood). Fig. 2 demonstrates behaviour patterns which occur as the wood dries out before you get it or, worse, after you have worked it! Sharp changes in grain direction can be seen – take them as a warning.

shrinkage cracks

good tangent cut

cupping

radial cut – large shrinkage

The shape of the component you cut will determine the strength. For example, a bracket will be of little supportive use when it is cut with much short grain it, whereas if you place the pattern so that the straight long grain passes through the area of greatest strain, the small amount of short grain will not drastically reduce its strength (Fig. 3).

Fig. 3

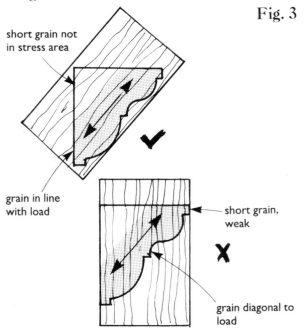

short grain not in stress area

grain in line with load

short grain, weak

grain diagonal to load

If you are faced with the task of edge-joining boards to make up a wide panel, look at the end grain. If it is laid out with the grain pattern alternating, each will try to cancel out warping or 'cupping' of the next. For areas where this is most important, such as solid table-tops, narrow alternated sections are glued up together, to provide a much greater resistance to warping. Fig. 4 explains. Most of the table and seat areas in these projects are slatted, to allow the wood to adjust itself without affecting the general shape markedly. Where the wood is used in plant containers, however, the structure has been designed to survive by not imposing additional stress on the wood. All wood in contact with soil filling has to be treated very thoroughly with high-quality preservative, which should be allowed to soak well into the grain. Water-based preservatives are out for smooth wood.

Fig. 4

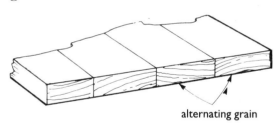

alternating grain

The outside can be coloured with stain preservative, which is also available with a gloss finish. The lighter shades of these allow the natural beauty of the grain to show through. There are microporous versions, and, of course, microporous paint for a white or colour finish. Microporous coatings allow the wood to breathe and adjust naturally, drying out if it gets wet. Ordinary paint will blister and flake if subjected to some of the treatment that garden woodwork has to contend with.

So, you see, the low-cost pine can have beauty and, with care, it may last a fair time, if not a lifetime. For that sort of endurance, you have to spend much more, and think of the cost of a mistake with teak or oak – the really traditional woods for garden structures and furniture.

MAKING JOINTS

All the joints for the projects in this book can be formed with hand-tools, but they can be made with less effort and more quickly with the help of an electric drill. Add power saws and a router for greater savings in time-consuming hand-work, and with practice the jobs should be more accurate.

BUTT JOINTS

Use this joint to create a wide surface from narrow material. You need cramps or wedges to assemble it. Its strength depends on the perfect match of two edges. If the timber is bought as PAR or PSE, then the edges should be true enough to match.

Nevertheless, the wood may have warped while in your care, so check that these are straight, level and at right angles to the face. Do this with a long steel rule or really straight metal strip and the try square. Place the boards together and hold them up to the light. Low spots will admit light. You then have to mark the dark high spots and plane or sand the high spots away until there is an even dark line (Fig. 1).

Fig. 1

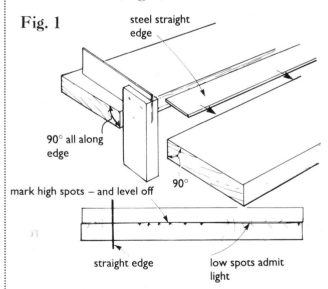

steel straight edge

90° all along edge

mark high spots – and level off

straight edge

low spots admit light

90°

When the edges are true, the boards should be level with each other; the straight edge laid across will prove this. Mark the joint edges with a face mark as shown, to indicate the corrected surface. This will ensure that they go together in the right position.

If the joint is a short one, there will be no need to do more than glue and cramp it, but if it is longer than 1 metre (3 ft 3 in), a dowel or two would not come amiss. To dowel such a joint, tape a household pin at the centre of the edge and press the other board on to it. The side of the pinhead will leave a mark on both edges. Drill for the dowel, usually 6 mm (¼ in), and glue in a hardwood dowel. Make a lengthwise sawcut in the dowel. This allows the air to escape, instead of pushing the glue out again (Fig. 2).

Use weatherproof glue and cramp the joint with sash cramps, or follow Fig. 3 and make an adaptor to fit a Workmate.

Fig. 2

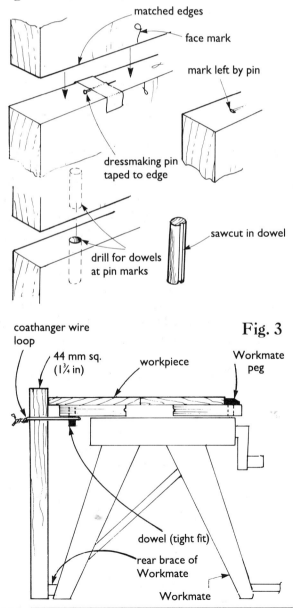

matched edges
face mark
mark left by pin
dressmaking pin taped to edge
drill for dowels at pin marks
sawcut in dowel

Fig. 3

coathanger wire loop
44 mm sq. (1¾ in)
workpiece
Workmate peg
dowel (tight fit)
rear brace of Workmate
Workmate

HALVING JOINTS

There are many of these in the various projects. Two strips of wood, usually of the same cross-section, are joined at a corner, crossing each other, forming a 'T' junction, or angled to each other.

All have one thing in common: a rebate or recess half its thickness, made to match the other piece of wood, which is also treated in the same way.

1 Lay the pieces of wood one over the other and mark the length, which should be the overall size in each piece, because of the overlap. Mark the width of the top piece on the bottom one, then scribe a line half-way down to set the depth of the rebate.

Use a marking knife and try square for right-angle joins and a sliding bevel for those that are angled. Make the marks with a marking knife (Fig. 1).

Fig. 1

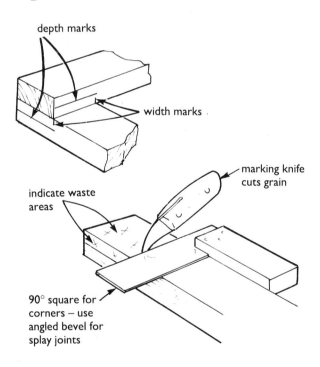

depth marks
width marks
marking knife cuts grain
indicate waste areas
90° square for corners – use angled bevel for splay joints

2 Using a chisel, form a groove across the wood against the knife cut on the waste side (Fig. 2). This will later guide a tenon saw and prevent it wandering on to the wrong side of the line.

Fig. 2

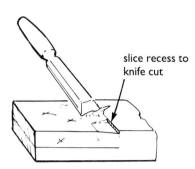

slice recess to
knife cut

3 Clamp the wood upright in the vice and saw down from the end to the waste side of the 'halving' line. Start with the saw at 45 degrees on the corner, then, as the cut progresses, level the saw to horizontal, as in Fig. 3. Stop at the cross-line. If you go very slightly past it, the wood will not be unduly weakened but the mark will show.

Fig. 3

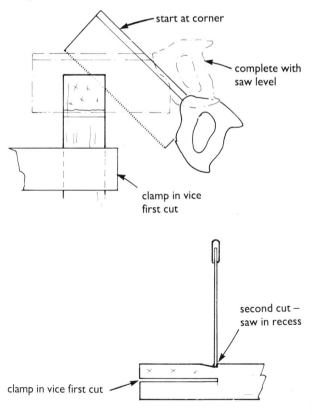

start at corner

complete with
saw level

clamp in vice
first cut

second cut –
saw in recess

clamp in vice first cut

4 Lay the wood on the bench hook, or clamp it in the Workmate. Rest the saw against the knife cut and in the chiselled recess of the waste, and cut carefully until

the waste is freed. Now stop. Any further and you will weaken the wood. If you had made this cut first, there would be a fair chance of going too far. This time the waste is on the 'safe' side of the first cut you made. Tidy up the surface with gentle strokes of a chisel held flat to remove saw marks only, down to the line.

5 Use the cut piece to mark the second piece, as in Fig. 4. Then follow Steps 2 to 4 again. Glue the joint only when all others on the same pieces of wood have been cut and tried for fit.

Fig. 4

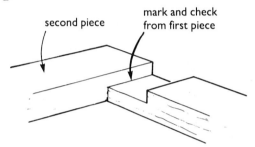

second piece

mark and check
from first piece

6 You can use woodscrews to reinforce and clamp the joints. If you do this, pre-plan by drilling for the screws with the joint held together dry. If you drill through wet glue, it makes a real mess of the drill bit. Polyester or epoxy resin is difficult to clean off.

If you just cramp them, remember to insert waste packing scraps of wood under the cramps to avoid marking the wood. If you put strips of plastic tape each side of the glue line, and polythene over the packing first, any glue escaping will not bond the packing wood to the job, or get on the outside of the joint (Fig. 5).

Fig. 5

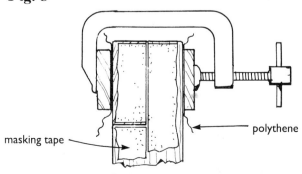

masking tape

polythene

MORTISE AND TENON

A mortise is a recess in one piece of wood and a tenon is a part of the end of the other which has been cut down in section to fit. Several types of mortise and tenon that are used in the projects are shown in Fig. 1.

Fig. 1

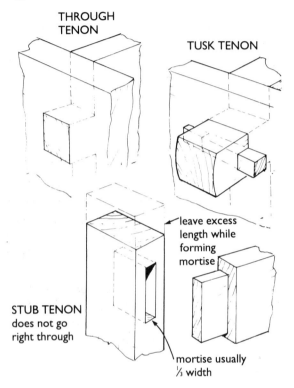

THROUGH TENON

TUSK TENON

leave excess length while forming mortise

STUB TENON does not go right through

mortise usually ⅓ width

The through tenon goes right through the other piece and may be made to grip by inserting wedges in its end. An extended type goes through far enough to have a hole cut in itself, and a wedge-shaped peg inserted. This is a pegged 'tusk' tenon.

Short tenons do not go right through, so they are not seen at all. These are 'stub' tenons and have to fit in a blind mortise. Tenons can be pulled in tight by using a tapered temporary peg (Fig. 2). Remove it when the glue has reached the rubbery state or it will be difficult to get out. Leaving the wedging dowel in the joint may appear structurally sound but, in fact, it does not help much at its thin end. In any case, both ends may be visible.

Clear the hole later, fit a new plain peg put in with fresh glue, and trim it flush with a sharp chisel held flat.

Fig. 2

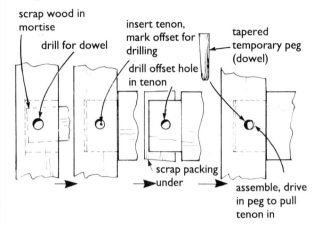

scrap wood in mortise

drill for dowel

insert tenon, mark offset for drilling

drill offset hole in tenon

tapered temporary peg (dowel)

scrap packing under

assemble, drive in peg to pull tenon in

The cutting of tenons is similar to the forming of a halving joint, except that some have to be shaped on three, or even four, faces.

Most woodworkers will make the tenon first, then mark the position of the mortise from it. However, some pieces have to be formed with the mortises in line with each other. Then the marking is transferred to the tenon part.

1 Mark out the mortise using the marking gauge with its pins set to the thickness of the intended tenon. It is convenient to make this, say, 9 mm (⅜ in), to suit the size of a router cutter when the mortise is deep and narrow, or to the thickness of the wood when simple mortises are made (as with the Trundle Seat, see page 70). To mortise with hand-tools, follow this sequence.

2 Mark out and drill a series of holes no wider than the mortise. If the mortise is not a through type, fit a depth gauge to the drill, or use a small block of wood on the drill to limit the depth.

Using a chisel (the 'firmer' type is best), chop cross-grain to remove the waste. Start at the furthest end and work back, away from the face of the chisel, as in Fig. 3. Shave the sides clean but do not go over the marked lines.

Where the tenon is to have wedges, as in a through tenon, the ends of the mortise need to be widened on the outside edge, as in Fig. 4. This is to allow the tenon to spread

Fig. 3

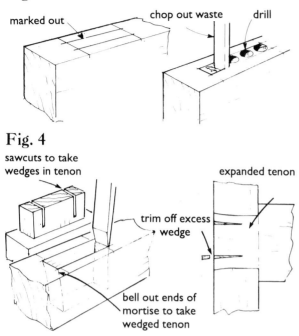

marked out — chop out waste — drill

Fig. 4

sawcuts to take wedges in tenon

expanded tenon

trim off excess wedge

bell out ends of mortise to take wedged tenon

out and grip the mortise when a wedge is inserted in the end of the tenon. Shave those ends carefully with the flat of the chisel.

Mortises can be formed with a router, provided that it will cut deeply enough. (See the section on power-tools, page 122.)

3 When the mortise is clean and true, check that the tenon fits. It should be firmly tight; if it needs force, shave it to fit.

DOVETAIL

This joint locks one piece into the other to resist an endwise pull. It is used on the Supertrug (see page 60) to hold the sides together. Fig. 1 shows the principle,

Fig. 1

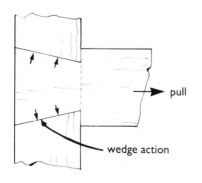

pull

wedge action

although it is only a single version of those generally used, for example, on drawer fronts. In this form, it is akin to a wedged tenon but open, or what is known as 'bare-faced'. In our application it is convenient to cut the end of the cross-piece to form the 'pin' first, then use it to mark the 'tail' recess in the other piece.

1 Mark out the shape to an angle of 15 degrees. Steeper angles will weaken the wood; gentler ones will reduce its holding power. The length of the joint will be equal to the thickness of the material to which it is joined.

2 Saw the pin sides in the same way as shown for making halving joints and tenons, using the tenon saw (Fig. 2). Mark the angles of the 'tail' from this, and mark a 'stop' line at the thickness of the pin. Saw down to this on the waste side of the first marks, then cut across near the stop line with a coping saw or jigsaw. Trim down to the line with a chisel and smooth and true up the sides until the pin fits firmly. Mark the joint for reference when gluing up, then continue with the other dovetails.

Fig. 2

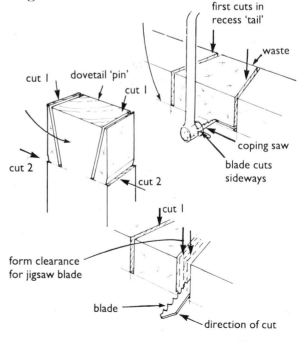

REBATED HOUSING

Wood is removed along its edge to accept the edge or end of another piece. Fig. 1 shows the application in these projects. Its purpose is to cover the edge of the piece it houses, to give two gluing areas and cover end grain.

In the projects, it holds the bottom panels in place.

Fig. 1

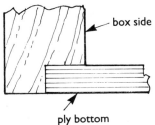

box side

ply bottom

APPLICATION

Traditionally, the rebate is cut with a rebate plane, which has an adjustable fence and a narrow blade. This is a fairly slow process. You also form it by making two cuts with small circular saw, equipped with a fence. Fig. 2 shows the sequence. Alternatively, you can use a router.

Fig. 2

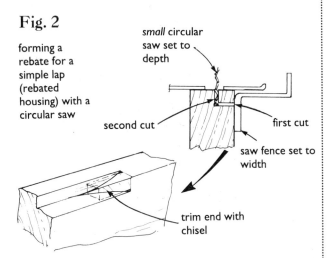

forming a rebate for a simple lap (rebated housing) with a circular saw

small circular saw set to depth

second cut

first cut

saw fence set to width

trim end with chisel

NAIL FIXINGS

The various types of nail are shown in Fig. 1. Of these the oval types are most widely used in these projects. They are less likely to split the wood and can be 'clenched' (bent over to secure at the back) easily.

Never nail where grain is short, or very

Fig. 1

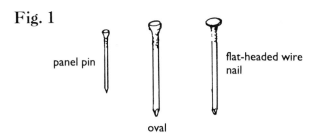

panel pin

oval

flat-headed wire nail

close to an end or edge. If you first hold the nail, head down, on a hard surface, then tap the point with the hammer to blunt it a little, it will cut its way through the fibres, rather than squeezing them apart and thus splitting the wood.

To be extra safe, particularly with thin wood near an end, or when larger nails are used, pre-drill the hole in the piece that is being nailed on.

Oval nails can be punched just below the surface, so that they can be filled over. A nail punch is shown in Fig. 2. If the nails are not near an end, you can try 'secret nailing'.

Fig. 2

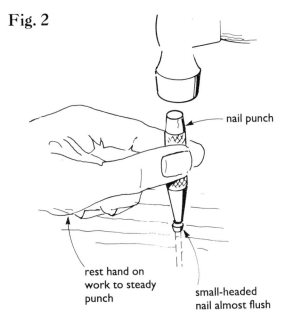

nail punch

rest hand on work to steady punch

small-headed nail almost flush

First, cut a shaving and prise it up to remain still attached at one end. Hammer the nail in as far as you can without hitting the shaving, then use a nail punch to drive it down into the recess. Glue the shaving down again, as in Fig. 3. If the secret fixing is near the end, be sure to make the shaving cut away from the end, or the shaving may break off.

You can hold small pieces in position with a panel pin, while glue sets. This thin,

Fig. 3

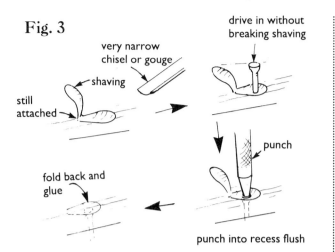

very narrow
chisel or gouge

shaving

still
attached

drive in without
breaking shaving

fold back and
glue

punch

punch into recess flush

almost headless, pin can be punched well down, whereas flat-headed nails cannot be hidden.

Should a nail start to go in crooked or bend, stop and pull it out, either with the claw of the hammer or with nail pullers or pincers. Place a scrap of packing on the wood to protect it and raise the hammer or puller as the nail is extracted (Fig. 4).

Fig. 4

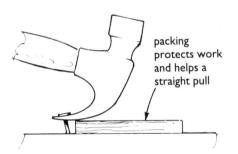

packing
protects work
and helps a
straight pull

SCREW FIXINGS

The various types of woodscrew are shown in Fig. 1.

Each screw is given a number according to its diameter, plus the length. Low numbers are thin, high numbers are thick. You use thicker screws when there is a high load on a screw which goes through the wood it is fixing into a thin piece. It is useless to have the threaded part mostly in the part that it passes right through and little in the piece to which it is fixed. Some have threads to the head. These require that pressure be put on the wood as the screw

Fig. 1

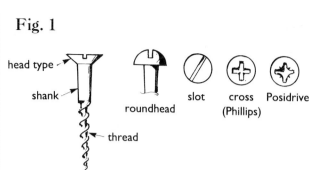

head type

shank

thread

countersunk

roundhead

slot

cross
(Phillips)

Posidrive

meets the second piece. Then the thread in the first piece helps to force the screw into the second.

There are several head types.

THE PLAIN SLOT

Here care is needed to keep the screwdriver central, for it will mark the wood if it creeps outside the edge of the head.

THE PHILLIPS TYPE

This has a cross-shaped hole. It needs a screwdriver of the same pattern to locate without slipping out.

THE POSIDRIVE

This is also cross-shaped, but at a different taper, so it needs a driver to match. Using the wrong driver chews up the head, and wears cheap screwdrivers.

A countersunk screw (csk) needs to have a conical counter-bore made in the pre-drilled hole. Hand-tools will suffice, but bits are made for electric drills to speed things up. Do not get carried away, or the hole will finish too large and the screw head will be surrounded by a hollow (Fig. 2). If you have a drill stand, raise the height adjustment, so that the bit bottoms at the right depth of

Fig. 2

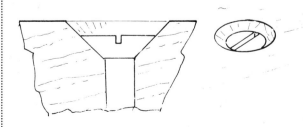

countersink. Drill a 'pilot hole' through both pieces of wood, first with a drill bit the same diameter as the threaded part, *less* the thickness of the threads. If it is too large, the threads will not bite in deeply enough. If it is too small, the screw will be too stiff to drive in. Next, drill the first piece of wood to clear the screw. Failure to do this will cause the screw to bind, and it may prevent the joint closing tightly.

When a thick piece is to be fixed, you can use a screw that is shorter than the whole joint. What is required is that the piece you are fixing should have enough wood under the head to be strong. The trick is 'counter-boring' (Fig. 3). Drill an even larger hole now, to clear the screw head through to a reasonable holding thickness – say, 25 mm (1 in). The drill bit will leave a counter-sinking recess for the head at the same time.

Fig. 3

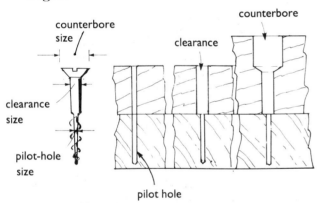

The right-size screwdriver will go into the hole and the screw will be hidden. You can also plug the hole after with a dowel. Screws which have to be hidden are dealt with in a similar way, as Fig. 4 explains.

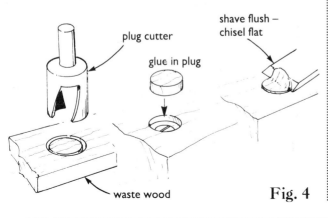

Fig. 4

GLUE JOINTS

Before you start gluing, make sure that all screw holes are drilled. You can use screws to clamp a joint only while the glue is wet. If you drill through wet glue, the drill bit will be covered in the stuff. It sets quickly as the drill becomes hotter, is difficult to get off, and the joint will be setting (curing) while you are fiddling with the drill!

All the glued joints in the projects are made with weatherproof glue. There are several types.

PVA WOODWORKERS' EXTERIOR WHITE GLUE

This is waterproof, but not entirely weatherproof. That depends on the joint fitting very well. It is not gap-filling. The joints have to be thoroughly sealed afterwards with an impermeable coating. It is suitable for joints where there is no mechanical movement, such as those held by screws or pegs or interlocking joints like tenons and dovetails.

UREA-FORMALDEHYDE (CASCAMITE)

This is a powder, to be mixed with water. When set, it is waterproof, but in severe weather it may lose strength in cavities. It is semi-transparent, and excess can be wiped away with a wet cloth before it sets. Cover it with impermeable paint or varnish.

RESORCINOL RESIN (CASCOPHEN)

This is a two-part glue which uses a catalyst to start curing. It is weatherproof and gap-filling. Clean off excess with water before it sets. You will need to wear gloves or use barrier cream when using it as the catalyst can cause dermatitis. It dries to a dark-red colour, so do not use under varnished work.

POLYESTER RESIN WITH CATALYST

This is weather-resistant and, when mixed, soaks well into the grain. If you warm it with a hair-dryer at this point, it spreads well. You have only about ten to fifteen minutes' working time between mixing and securing the joints, before the glue becomes jellified and refuses to allow the joint to be adjusted. Get your fixing screws in before this.

When set (cured) some hours after, it is almost transparent, but you can mix it with sawdust and use it to form fillets and as general filling. Clean the mixing tub and spreader with cellulose thinners before it hardens. Wear gloves or use barrier cream to protect against the effects of the catalyst. The car-repair section of DIY shops is a good source of supply.

EPOXY RESIN AND CATALYST

This is even more weather-resistant, but also more expensive. It can double up as a varnish too. There is a thixotropic additive which you can mix in to prevent it running out of the joint and fillers to span gaps (not that a good joint has any). It also cures almost clear.

All the project prototypes were made with the polyester resin/catalyst (hardener) glue, as recommended for glassfibre work. Here are a few tips in its use.

MIXING

Mix only enough for immediate assembly.

Do a dummy run with a couple of joints, dry, and time yourself. Add a minute or two for fumbles. Did you remember to drill for screws?

Measure the resin into a clean paper cup and squeeze out the recommended quantity of catalyst (hardener) on to a lolly stick or piece of scrap wood. Mix in thoroughly until a uniform shade is achieved in the resin. You can mix small quantities on a paper saucer – it is easier to blend.

Apply to one surface of the joint, but all over its various meeting faces. Bring the joint together and screw it or nail it.

In cold weather the resin is stiff. You can make it spread easily by using a hair-dryer on the wood before you start.

Never try to spread the glue once it has reached a slightly rubbery stage. It is curing already. This happens more quickly in hot weather. You can delay this point by putting the mixing dish over a bowl of ice cubes.

When gluing sloping joints such as a scarf, or where the wood is tapered, the glue will try to slide. Stop its tricks by driving a panel pin in first, so that its point just projects into the joint (Fig. 1). This grips the other piece and prevents it sliding when the glue is spread.

Fig. 1

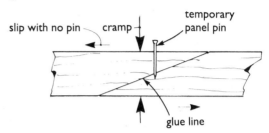

MASKING

There are areas where glue might prevent a wood stain soaking in, so cover those parts with masking tape before applying glue to the joint proper (Fig. 2).

Fig. 2

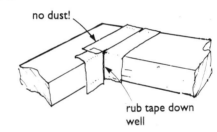

CRAMPING

Carpenter's 'G' cramps will suffice for holding those joints that are not additionally held with woodscrews. Place packing scraps of wood to protect the surface under the head and screw ends of the cramp. Sash cramps will hold wide panels and large jobs like door frames. A length of stout batten may well serve when adapted as in Fig. 3.

Fig. 3

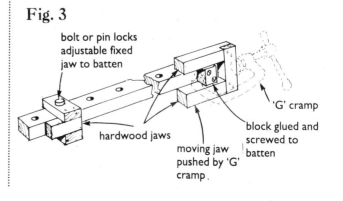

Power-tool Tips

Fig. 1

Electric Drill

The drill probably gets the most work to do, so choose one that is man enough to last through other DIY tasks besides these projects. The prototypes of the examples here were constructed with the aid of a 9-mm-capacity (⅜-in) reversible drill with speed and torque control, plus hammer action. This was also used to drive screws.

The following basic rules apply to all mains power-tools.

- Lay the cable where it will not hamper the smooth movement of the tool.
- Keep the cable away from your feet, to avoid tripping while the tool is running. Also, if you do tread on the cable, it may jerk the drill and break the bit or score the job.
- Always stow the chuck key in the holder before switching on.
- Start at low speed to avoid a torque kick, which may put the drill out of line.
- Never try to correct a sloping hole by leaning the drill over when the drill bit is of a small diameter.
- Do not put the tool down until the motor has stopped.
- Do not leave it lying about with a drill bit in the chuck; the bit may get broken.
- Do not leave it plugged in.
- Clear sawdust from the cooling intake slots frequently, by brushing, not prodding.
- Do not let it get wet.
- Clamp small workpieces, so they are not moved by the action of the tool. Holding them in the hand is not safe – you can be injured, even when using a sander.
- Never clamp the tool directly in a vice. It may be damaged or it may come loose. Use the appropriate manufacturer's accessory to hold it properly and safely.

If the drill has a depth-gauge rod, this can be a guide to check that the drill is perpendicular to the job. Use a small set square or try square against it in two directions (Fig. 1). If you have a drill stand, this happens automatically, but it is not

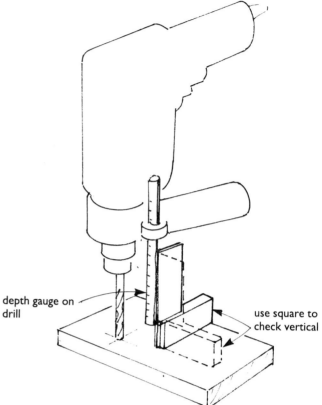

depth gauge on drill

use square to check vertical

always possible to fit the workpiece on to the stand. If you can, take advantage of the slots in the base to mount a clamp to hold the wood.

Some power-drills will not fit drill accessories of a different make, so try to choose the drill whose manufacturer has the accessories you will need.

Hand-held Circular Saw

Next to the power drill, this tool is probably the most used, and often the most abused, hand-power-tool. If there is a lot of work to do, try one with a 150-mm (6-in) minimum blade. Most saws have a combination woodwork blade. Different makes offer widely differing tooth forms, all of which work well when used correctly. Almost all have a tilt facility, depth control and a fence. All have a spring-back safety cover. Choose a model which has clearly seen alignment marks on the sole plate. The better-quality types have large, easy-to-adjust, clamp knobs, and extra hand-holds.

Familiarize yourself with its settings on a

scrap piece of wood before working on a project. This will show the width of the kerf and how far you have to slide it until the blade reaches the wood.

The hand-held saw scores in a confined space, whereas one in a sawbench needs more than twice the length of the wood for ripping, and almost the same in width for cross-cutting.

Always clamp the wood for ripping and use the saw level. If you try to hold it on its side, it will be less accurate, and probably unsafe.

Do not saw past side clamps; the wood will squeeze up and bind on the saw (Fig. 1). Turn it round and attack it from the other end.

Fig. 1

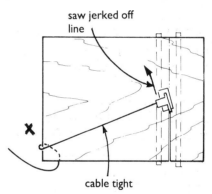

Large pieces and panels can be cut on the floor. Lay them on packing strips which go parallel to and fairly near the intended cutting line (Fig. 2). If you kneel on the

Fig. 2

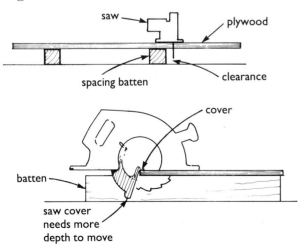

wood as you push the saw, your weight will hold it steady and cancel out the forward thrust you are putting on the saw. If you do not place your weight on it, then wedge an

end stop between the work and a wall or heavy object. The stop has to be longer than the sole plate of the saw, so that it can clear at the end of the cut (Fig. 3).

Fig. 3

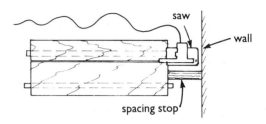

Mind that the cable does not become wedged in the sawcut or under the board. This could put it off course (Fig. 4).

Fig. 4

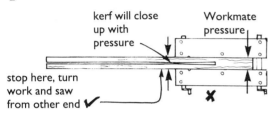

Keep the revs up. Saws are designed to cut at high speed, which allows the chips to clear quickly, so the blade stays fairly cool. If you force or twist it to correct the direction, it will overheat and slow, thus reducing the cooling action still further. It spoils the temper of the blade, which means that it will blunt and not hold a resharpened edge for long.

If the saw goes off the line, ease off and go back a little without twisting it (that would make the saw kick and you could lose control). Gently reinsert it on line and slowly guide it past the offending run-off. Always have full revs before making the cut.

Some portable saws can be mounted in specially designed tables so that they can be used for sawbench work. Never try to modify a tool that is not designed to be so mounted; you may find that it is difficult to adjust or is inaccurate when a fence is used.

JIGSAW

Choose the type which has variable speed and (if possible) orbital action, as this makes it easier to use; the blade returns clear of the wood, so it does not try to lift. All jigsaws cut on the upstroke against the sole plate, which may be tilted for angled cuts. Use fine-pitch blades for thin material and coarse for thick. The blade should cut around sharp curves, but ease off the forward pressure and allow the blade to cut itself a wider kerf here for turning clearance. Alternatively, back off and take a short angled cut to give it space on the waste side. Fig. 1 explains.

Fig. 1

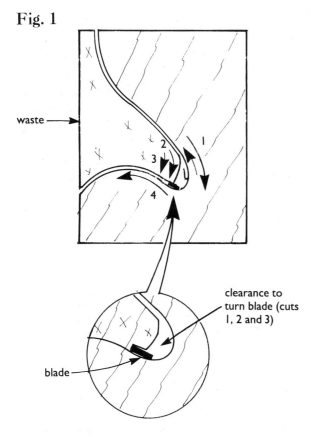

waste

clearance to turn blade (cuts 1, 2 and 3)

blade

ROUTER

A whole series of edge profiles can be formed with a router, and it will form grooves and slots, rebates, halving joints and mortises. Inside corners can have as small a radius as the cutter in use. These go down to 1.5 mm ($\frac{1}{16}$ in). But, of course, small cutters cut more slowly than those of a larger diameter. Fig. 1 shows the range of edges and recesses that you can cut just for the

Fig. 1

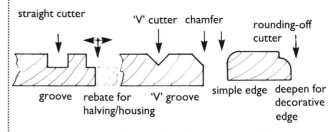

straight cutter · 'V' cutter · chamfer · rounding-off cutter

groove · rebate for halving/housing · 'V' groove · simple edge · deepen for decorative edge

projects in this book. A router will tackle many more.

The accessories that come with most routers enable them to use templates, take a cut that follows a curving edge and produce radiused cuts. You can make simple jigs and guides, to combine with some of these or to use directly with the router.

Routers have to run very fast, so you will need ear defenders and goggles. Never force them to cut faster or deeper than they will naturally. Heavy work slows them – the cutter overheats and the wood scorches. Keep that even whine going. Do not feed the cutter into the job before the speed has peaked and always cut on the advancing side of the cutter. This means that if you are cutting round the outside of a workpiece, you pull it towards you on the left-hand side of the wood and go counter-clockwise on all external edges. If you cut the centre out of a piece, go *clockwise*, so that the advancing side of the cutter is in the same direction as the cut. Study Fig. 2 and practise a few times in the air before switching on.

Fig. 2

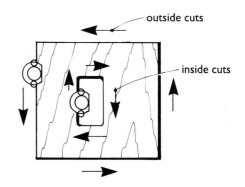

outside cuts

inside cuts

If you try to move the router the wrong way, the cutter will kick and try to walk along the line backwards, making a thorough mess of the job.

There are no such rules when you make a simple slot, but remember that deep slots have to be cut in stages, so as not to overload the router.

Always clamp the work and place a piece of scrap wood at the exit side or end, so that the cutter does not break out the grain (Fig. 3).

Fig. 3

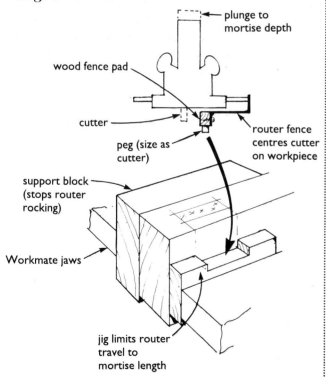

scrap piece for cutter run-out (prevents grain breaking out)

cramps to table or Workmate

workpiece

clamping batten (also use as a fence)

You can rout mortises with little more than a pre-shaped strip of wood clamped to the job and a peg in the sub-fence (Fig. 4).

Fig. 4

plunge to mortise depth

wood fence pad

cutter

peg (size as cutter)

router fence centres cutter on workpiece

support block (stops router rocking)

Workmate jaws

jig limits router travel to mortise length

Routed mortises have rounded ends, so either round the tenons to fit or square up the mortises with a chisel (Fig. 5).

Fig. 5

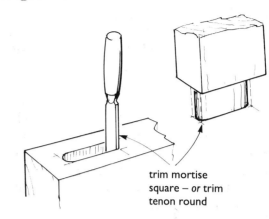

trim mortise square – *or* trim tenon round

POWER PLANE

This removes wood fast and, like most power-tools, has to be allowed to keep its revs up. A smoother cut results if you angle the tool as you push it (Fig. 1). This gives more of a slicing action. Although there will be a depth of cut adjustment, remember that this controls the front of the sole plate, and that a power plane is only as accurate as the user with a hand-plane. Hold it level or tilted as required to shape the wood evenly.

Fig. 1

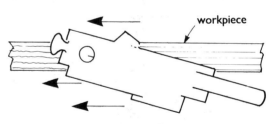

workpiece

As with hand-planes, apply more pressure at the front when entering the cut and more at the back as the cutter nears the finish. This is to avoid a hump in the middle of the cut, because the natural movement of the body is in an arc about your feet (Fig. 2).

Lay the plane on its side to avoid damaging the cutters.

Fig. 2

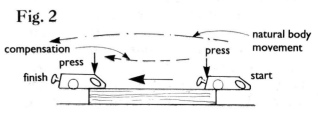

natural body movement

compensation

press

press

finish

start

BELT SANDER

Belt-sanding gives a more consistently level surface than you can get with a sanding disc on a drill, because it has a metal sole plate inside the belt. Although hand-held, it can also be mounted in a special clamp to transform it into a bench sander, working level or on its side, so that it can be used for squaring up edges and ends. It removes wood much faster than an orbital type, and with a fine grit belt gives a finishing grade of surface.

Keep a firm grip on it when hand-holding, because there is a lot of drag on the belt and it will try to leap forward. Do not hand-feed the corner of a piece of wood to it in the opposite direction to the belt, or it will kick the wood back at you (Fig. 1). Let it stroke the corner away with the grain, and watch your knuckles.

Fig. 1

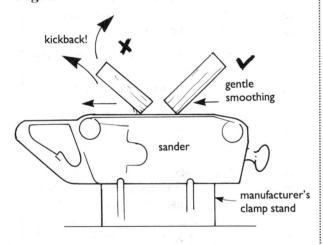

kickback!

gentle smoothing

sander

manufacturer's clamp stand

ORBITAL SANDER

This gets into corners that the belt job cannot reach, but if a piece of grit finds its way on to the sanding pad, it will leave a series of tiny circles on the wood. Brush that wood and the pad clean before working and do not park the pad on the floor. In order for the sander to do its job, the wood has to be firm or clamped. If it is a small, light or flexible piece, it will just wobble at high speed with the pad, make a lot of noise and not get sanded.

SHARPENING TOOLS

There are three stages in forming a good cutting edge: grinding to the right clearance angle, sharpening to a cutting edge and finally honing so that it is polished.

As bought, the clearance angle will have been ground to 20 degrees. Unless you have very old and worn tools, the grindstone will not be needed. Should it be necessary to regrind, use a power grinder and apply hardly any pressure. Otherwise the tip of the tool will get overheated and so lose the temper which enables it to hold its edge. If you see a blue tinge, then it is too late.

The cutting edge has to be at a slightly steeper slope; 25 degrees for softwoods and a little steeper for hardwoods. Use an oilstone for this. The stone usually has medium and smooth sides. It should fit in a wooden box to keep it firm and to protect it. Put a few drops of light oil on the surface and hold the tool at the correct angle (sharpening jigs are available; these clamp to the blade and roll along the stone). With practice you will be able to do it by eye and feel. Draw the blade towards you in an 'S' shape to cover the width of the stone. Let it glide back to complete a figure '8' without pressing. Do this a number of times until you can see or feel a slight ridge on the tip. This is called a burr.

Turn the blade on to the flat side and lay it on the stone. Draw it backwards only to remove the burr. You will see bits of it drop off on to the stone. Do not break them off by hand.

This is quite a sharp edge, but not keen or smooth enough. Do it again on the smooth side of the stone until a new burr appears. Remove it as before, then do it yet again with less pressure. If you can see from the surface of the stone that the path it leaves is smooth and even, then go to the next stage. If there are ridges of oil and stone slurry, then you will find little nicks in the edge of the blade. Keep on sharpening until the edge is straight and level (see Fig. 1).

If you indulge in much woodwork you

Fig. 1

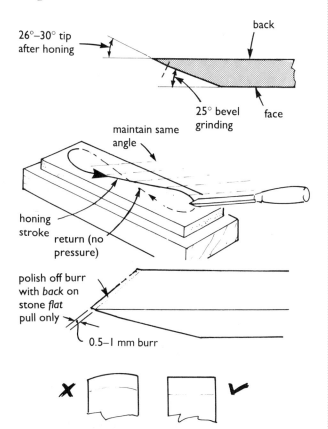

26°–30° tip after honing

back

25° bevel grinding

face

maintain same angle

honing stroke

return (no pressure)

polish off burr with *back* on stone *flat* pull only

0.5–1 mm burr

✗ ✓

will do well to invest in a slow-speed water stone. This gives a superior edge and keeps the tool cool, right at the very tip where you cannot tell that it is getting too hot.

Now for the final polishing that will make the blade slide through the wood with little effort and leave a smooth cut. Use a leather strop or wheel facing for this. Apply a little honing compound to the leather and burnish the back and front of the tool, stroking away from the tip. Do the front five times to one stroke on the back. This avoids changing the angles. A high polish should result. Do not get carried away, however, or the edge may be polished to a different shape.

As you use the tool, be it chisel or plane iron, give it a strop or two at regular intervals.

Blunt chisels are difficult to control. They move jerkily and leave torn fibres and score marks. You are more likely to cut yourself, because a blunt chisel does not go where you direct it.

SAFETY TIPS

When you put down a chisel, place its handle towards you, where you can see it. If the blade gets covered with shavings which you then brush away with your hand, there is less chance of cutting your hand if the whole chisel is not buried in shavings.

Make sure that the rack where you keep chisels or saws is positioned high enough and protected below, so that your hands will not be near the blade ends as you work.

Wear stout shoes, rather than sandals or trainers, to protect your feet if sharp or heavy objects fall from the bench.

If you have removed a piece of wood which was nailed, take the nail out before it is forgotten. This will prevent possible damage to you, your clothes or other work.

Do not hang heavy items high on the wall. They cause more havoc the further they fall.

Wind up loose cables so that they do not tangle. Tangled cables catch and hamper the movement of power tools.

Position your power sockets in such a way that any cables that are plugged in will be clear of the working area of the bench.

Clearly mark each plug with the name of each tool. That way you can quickly see if a particular tool is still plugged in.

Never turn the workshop power off until you have unplugged those power tools that have normal switches or triggers that have locking-on buttons. If a tool is left switched on and plugged into a 'dead' socket, it will start up when the power supply is switched on.

You may wear a dust-mask while working with a power tool. Also remember to wear it when you sweep the floor. It's a good idea to use a vacuum cleaner as an added precaution against dust.

You may have an allergic reaction to some types of weatherproof glue. For protection, wear goggles and plastic gloves, use barrier cream around the nostrils and work outside or in a well-ventilated area.

INDEX